Searching For Spirits

The Ultimate Guide for Ghost Hunters

Searching For Spirits

The Ultimate Guide for Ghost Hunters

By
Kalila Smith

Searching For Spirits

Cover design by Allan Gilbreath

This is a work of memory, personal point of view, and storytelling. The names, characters, places, and incidents are known publicly, are common knowledge, or are used only from a memoir point of view. All opinions and events related are told from the author's point of view.

Published by
Dark Oak Press
Kerlak Enterprises, Inc.
Memphis, TN
www.darkoakpress.com

ISBN 13: 978-1-937035-71-6
Library of Congress Control Number: 2014938736
First Printing: 2014

Special thanks to everyone at Dark Oak Press for all of the encouragement and assistance.

This book is printed on acid free paper.

Printed in the United States of America

Dedication:

Dedicated in loving memory to my beloved daughter, Stephanie; you were part of everything I did; you will always be my special angel. And to my cherished friend, Gary; thank you for your inspiration.

Acknowledgements

Thanks to everyone who contributed to the investigations, interviews, and experiences that made this book possible. Thanks to Dr. Raymond Buckland for your infinite wisdom and knowledge and for the wonderful demon box, that I had so much fun with. Thanks to Anna Parmalee of Erzulie's Authentic Voudou for reminding me of things I might forget and for your wonderful products that I use in conjunction with my work with spirits. Pat Fitzhugh for the experience with the Bell Witch. And to: Allan Gilbreath, Megan Edmonds, and the paranormal crew at PRIA in Memphis for assisting in the investigation at Natchez.

Table of Contents

Preface

In Fall 2001, the University of New Orleans proposed an opportunity for me to teach a class in their non-credit Metropolitan College. The class was called "Haunted History of New Orleans". The intent was to offer locals an offbeat history lesson that introduced them to the darker side of New Orleans. It became an instant success. For the following three years, I took groups of eager "students" on a journey into New Orleans' seedy history, ghost stories, legends, and paranormal investigations. My students consisted of everyone from housewives to judges, college students to doctors. It was obvious that people from all lifestyles were curious not only about history but in the paranormal as well. The class discontinued in 2005 due to Hurricane Katrina.

After Katrina, I received emails from individuals inquiring about the continuation of the class. Unfortunately, Hurricanes Gustav and Ike, both of which struck only twelve days apart in early August, hindered interest when the University attempted to offer the program again in the August 2008 enrollment. The university never attempted to revive the class again.

This book is a collection of notes, experiments, and case studies from the original UNO class. Throughout the years, I have added my personal experiences and conclusions from various investigations conducted for television shows and documentaries. The purpose of this book is to provide seekers of the unknown a concise guide to the world of spirits.

Introduction

Life continuing after death has intrigued mankind since the dawn of time. Every culture and every religion has had some form of belief in an afterlife. Early civilizations built great tombs and temples to pay homage to the dead. The ancient Egyptians buried their dead with treasures. Servants were often killed and buried along with them to continue to serve kings in the afterlife. Ancient religions always included gods and goddesses who ruled the spirit world. The ancient Egyptians believed that danger lurked in the Underworld. Papyrus scrolls, popularly known as Books of the Dead, contained the powerful spells and images necessary to ensure a safe journey through the afterlife.

This belief is common in many other early cultures and religions. They believed that in order to get to the afterlife, they would have to pass through a dangerous place filled with monsters, boiling lakes, fires, and poisonous snakes. These evils could be overcome with the right spells. If they overcame the evils they would reach the gates of Yaru (the Egyptian afterlife) and meet loved ones again, but first they had to pass the greatest test of all in the Hall of Two Truths. This test involved weighing the heart, the only organ left in the body. The heart was placed on one side of a balance and on the other side, the Feather of Truth which held all the lies and sins of their past life. The three great gods, Osiris, Anubis, and Thoth, decided the result of the weighing. If the heart passed the test then the deceased was allowed to enter the gates of Yaru. However if the heart failed the test then a terrifying monster known as the Devourer ate it. The Devourer was part crocodile, part hippopotamus, and part lion. Once it had eaten a heart the dead person was gone forever.

In ancient Greece, Hades ruled the Underworld. Souls were guided to the River Styx that stood between the world of the living and that of the dead. Charon crossed the soul over to the other side where it would be judged by Hades and sent to either a paradise or an eternity of punishment. Certain heroes in Greek mythology often had to enter the Underworld to prove their bravery to the gods. Hades interacted with both the dead and the living. One of the most popular tales of Hades is when he fell in love with the goddess Persephone, daughter of Demeter and Zeus. Hades rose from the Underworld as the innocent maiden picked flowers in a field. He raped and abducted her, hiding her away in the world of the dead. Demeter eventually learned of her daughter's fate and refused to allow crops to grow on the earth until he returned her daughter.

Zeus eventually intervened, forcing Hades to return the girl to the living, but before he did this,

Hades tricked her into eating some pomegranate seeds in the Underworld. By doing this, she doomed herself to remain in the land of the dead, for if anyone ate there, they must stay. Finally, it was agreed that she would only have to spend part of the year in the Underworld and the rest of the year with her mother in the physical world. This story seems to explain the seasons and the cycle of the crops, but it is proof that the belief in a spirit world that paralleled our living world existed long before now.

Eastern religions brought purpose into the afterlife. Eastern cultures believed that the soul is immortal because that is its nature, having been created by God. Life repeats itself through earthly incarnations, which allow the soul to learn lessons and work towards God's consciousness. Most of these cultures continue to honor their dead with altars and offerings, and each had some form of belief that the dead would remain nearby to protect and give counsel. In modern culture, we have elaborate funerals and memorial services to say our goodbyes to our loved ones while sending them off to the other side knowing they are loved and remembered. We remember the dead by bringing flowers to gravesites on special occasions. In New Orleans, there was a French tradition to not only bring flowers to honor the souls of the dead on All Saints Day, November 1, but to have a picnic in the cemetery to feast with the dead.

October 31, Halloween as we know it, is often considered a time when the veil between our world and the spirit world is the thinnest. The following day is celebrated in many cultures as a day to honor the dead.

Early Christian doctrines began considering the need to purify the soul. The Medieval church embellished on the once traditional ideology of the afterlife. Hades developed into a fiery Hell. Heaven and Hell became eternal. Eternal life was attainable only through God's Grace.

The Roman Catholic Church later added a temporary place where one could purify their soul and attain entry into the eternal heaven: *purgatory*. The Catholic Church believed that all humans were born with *original sin*, put upon us by Adam and Eve. Then we have *mortal sins;* these are the sins we acquire during our life. Those who were free of original sin through baptismal and free of their mortal sins through forgiveness of God would enter into the eternal bliss of heaven. Those who died having not paid penance for *venial sins*, lesser sins, could pay their penance in the afterlife in a place called *purgatory*. The Latin word *purgare* means to make clean or to purify. A soul could spend time in purgatory and work their way to eternal heaven. Another afterlife destination appointed by the Catholic Church is *limbo*. Limbo is a place of abode for those souls never baptized. But what exactly is a soul?

A soul is what animates the physical body. It is what makes us conscious. It is that part of the self that connects to a higher consciousness or God. In many traditions, it is believed that we are connected on that spirit level to one Great Spirit in the cosmos.

In traditional Chinese Medicine, it is believed that all pain and disease in the body stem initially from dysfunction in the *'Shen'*, or *spirit*. Again, this belief pops up in other ancient traditions. A disconnection of the spirit from its creator or source was believed to cause discord in both mind and body. Emotional imbalances stemmed from spiritual imbalances that eventually manifested into physical illness. In most early cultures, there was a distinct connection between spirituality and medicine. In early African religions, the physicians and herbalists were also the priests and priestesses. Those who healed the body and mind also healed the spirit.

As modern man evolved, he seemed to have lost his connection with spirit. Views on death and the afterlife changed. People began to fear death rather than accept it as a part of life.

The Age Of Spiritualism

In the Victorian era, Europeans and Americans alike cultivated an obsession with *spiritualism*, or communication with the dead. The Webster's dictionary defines Spiritualism as: "the belief that the dead survive as spirits that can communicate with the living, especially with the help of a third party, called a medium." The definition adopted in 1948, during the movement known as Modern Spiritualism, very succinctly defines Spiritualism as "the proof of survival".

During the Victorian Era, obsession with death turned into fashion as communication with the dead became a favorite pastime as well as a dark form of entertainment. Death during the Victorian age was not taken lightly. Elaborate rituals were held to send off the dead in style. Even the poorest of them sacrificed comforts of the living to save for funeral expenses. The ritual began with a three or four day wake. The body of the deceased would be set out in a coffin in the parlor for all to visit and pay their last respects. A family member or neighbor would be in charge of sitting with the dead throughout the waking period. The main reason for the wake period, of course, was to insure that the dead were really dead. Bodies were not embalmed at that time and it was necessary to make sure that the presumed deceased wasn't merely in a coma. Some coffins were left open; others had a glass viewing port to allow viewing of the corpse in a closed casket. Curtains remained drawn and a wreath made with black crepe would be set on the front door for all to see that death had visited the home. The custom of flowers and candles surrounding the coffin began as an attempt to quell the odors of death. Friends and family members sent gifts and food to the family.

This was a time of great superstition. Clocks were stopped at the time of death to keep bad luck away. Mirrors were covered with black cloth to prevent the spirits of the dead from being trapped inside. It is interesting to note at this point that many ghost photos are captured inside reflections in mirrors. Perhaps there was some substance to that fear. Most superstitions were based on fear and lack of knowledge of the disease, death, and decomposition process. Certainly some had to have some factual basis. Something provoked these concepts in order for people to have so much fear about them.

Other superstitions included never speaking ill of the dead in fear that they would return to haunt. If rain fell during a funeral, they would consider it a good omen; the spirit was bound for heaven. However, it was bad luck for the family if the rain fell into an open grave. A loud clap of thunder during the burial symbolized the soul was being received in heaven. It was considered bad luck to run into a funeral procession.

Birds were often associated with being the harbingers of doom, owls especially. To see an owl during the day or hear its hoot signified that someone would soon die. If a bird hit or flew into the glass window, it was also a death omen. Two deaths in a family always foretold of a third to come.

After the wake period, the funeral ritual began. Invitations went out to friends and family announcing the death and the funeral arrangements. Obituary notices were made public.

Family members had to wear a certain type of mourning wear for a required period of time. Widows were required to wear black for one year and a day. The extra day was meant to surpass the actual anniversary of the death. Other family members wore black, but the amount of time varied depending on the relationship to the deceased. Children usually wore white trimmed in black. Veils covered the faces of those in mourning for two reasons. The first was to hide the tears of the mourner and the second based more on superstition than practicality.

It was believed that the spirit of the dead hovered around loved ones and that if one looked upon the face of the mourner, the spirit could attach to the onlooker.

The funeral procession was drawn by the hearse coach with several horses with ostrich plumes of black upon their heads. The coffin lay inside covered in flowers.

The family and other mourners followed in carriages moving at a slow pace to the chapel and then the burial location. The wealthy often hired professional mourners to attend the ceremony who followed the procession wearing black and crying for the dead. Women were often spared witnessing the actual internment. Bricking over the grave was common practice to prevent grave robbing. A morbid fear of being buried alive prompted many to have a bell attached to a chain that led into the coffin itself.

In the event of a mistake and one awoke from a coma, the presumed dead could ring the bell from the grave and be rescued. This of course is where the terms "dead ringer" and "saved by the bell" were attained. After the burial, a great feast was served at the home of the family.

No doubt, the most macabre practice of the Victorians was the post-mortem photograph. Photography was popular during this period and taking photos of the dead was an obsession.

Families routinely photographed the dead loved one in their coffin or posed with other family members. It was particularly popular to immortalize a deceased child in this way. Some families even had the photos put on the funeral invitations. Once the deceased were finally at rest, many a Victorian commenced with attempts to communicate with the dearly departed.

Séances were commonly held to assist the family of the deceased communicate with their loved ones. During a séance, a group of individuals were seated at a table, held hands, and asked questions of the spirits. The spirits answer through knocks, raps, or tipping the table. More advanced forms of the séance incorporate the use of a medium that channels the spirits. Early mediums also claimed to produce *ectoplasm*, or ghostly fog like matter, that expressed from their noses, ears, and mouths. Early photographs showed mediums with a white solid substance oozing out their orifices.

Although I have never personally experienced this phenomenon, I have seen it occur in modern times. A photograph taken at Witchfest 2002 depicted renowned author and practitioner, Ed Fitch, conducting a ritual. In the photograph, ectoplasm was seen extending from him.

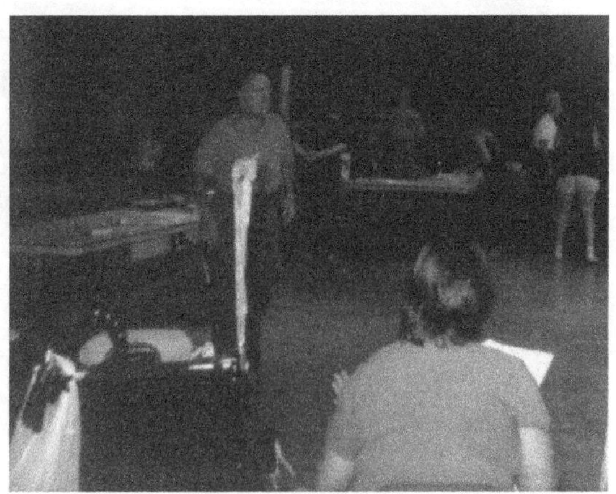

In "The History of Spiritualism," by Arthur Conan Doyle, the first spiritualist, Emanuel Swedenborg (1688-1772) was outlined. Swedenborg was the first European to popularize the idea that communication was possible with spiritual beings other than those of a higher order. He was the first to note that there were various planes to the spirit realm.

Clairvoyant Andrew Jackson Davis (1826-1910) was credited with being the father of Modern Spiritualism. He grew up impoverished in Blooming Grove, New York, the son of a shoemaker. He became interested in mesmerism (hypnotism) and through attending seminars on the subject discovered that in a trance state one could diagnose medical disorders in others. Through his mind's eye in an altered state, he could literally see through the physical body and directly at organs inside.

In 1844, he experienced an out of body trance state and found himself 40 miles away in the Catskills Mountains. It was there that he envisioned the apparitions of the philosopher Galen and the Swedish seer Emanuel Swedenborg, both of whom were dead.

This bizarre experience had a great impact on Davis. He began to travel giving lectures on the subject of spiritualism. It was through these travels that he met Dr. Lyons and Rev. Fishboug. Dr. Lyons was a renowned mesmerist who began a series of trance sessions on Davis. In the trance state, Davis dictated "The Principles of Nature: Her Divine Revelations and A Voice To Mankind".

The process took fifteen months to complete. Due to his lack of education, it was presumed that Davis was truly channeling from a higher source, perhaps even Swedenborg himself. "Principles of Nature" was published in 1847. He went on to write over 30 books on the subject. He eventually obtained a medical degree and retired in Boston.

In 1848, Margaretta and Kate Fox were the first in America to popularize spirit tapping as a form of communication with the dead. They claimed to communicate with the spirit of man named Charles B. Rosna. The spirit conveyed to the sisters that he had been murdered and buried in the basement of their home.

The family had moved to the house in December of the previous year and the house was reputed being haunted by the previous owner. In March of 1848, the family began to experience loud noises in the house such that the beds shook.

The sisters began to communicate with the spirit by asking it to repeat rapping sounds that they made. In time, they used these raps to ask particular questions of the spirit. In 1904, *The Boston Journal* confirmed that the skeletal remains of a man had been found buried beneath the basement of the house. I learned from a friend, renowned expert on spirit communication Dr. Raymond Buckland, that along with the remains was a tin box that belonged to the man. It is on display in the Lily Dale Museum in New York. There is a photo of the box in Dr.

Buckland’s book, “Buckland's Book of Spirit Communications”.

It was also during this early part of the 1900s that famed illusionist and escape artist Harry Houdini became interested in spiritualism. His interest sparked from the death of his mother. Houdini went to great lengths, visiting mediums and attending séances, in attempts to communicate with his her.

When his efforts failed, he became convinced that many spiritualists were charlatans and set out to expose them. He spent the last thirteen years of life debunking mediums.

Using his knowledge of illusions, he was able to duplicate ghostly images in photographs, along with the sounds and dramatic table tipping of early séances.

It is interesting to note that early spirit photography depicted full-bodied apparitions that are rarely seen in photographs today. It is hard to believe that apparitions appeared so easily on early photos when today’s technology rarely captures them.

Houdini’s work uncovered many an unethical charlatan. No doubt, much of the spiritualism rave of the Victorian era was more entertainment rather than actual contact with the other side.

Not all spiritualists were fakes, however. Many were truly dedicated to the cause of proving that life continued to exist after death.

It was also in the latter part of the eighteenth century that Madame Helen P. Blavatsky began her teachings on Theosophy. The word translated from Greek to mean "Divine Wisdom." The principles of Theosophy dealt with "the unity of life, the law of cycles, and the progressive consciousness in all kingdoms of nature (both visible and invisible)". Madame Blavatsky taught of the origins of life and of death. These teachings included the dual doctrine of karma and reincarnation.

Her teachings combined Eastern as well as Western philosophies to explain man's existence and continued existence on other planes. Her belief system incorporated that of early animistic beliefs that all life is connected throughout the cosmos. According to Blavatsky, everything in the universe is connected to everything else. All are connected to a Divine energy.

Regardless of one's beliefs, it is inevitable that we will all leave our physical bodies and what we call our spirits or souls will go somewhere else. The problem is that even for the most devoted believers, no one really knows for sure what happens to us after death.

Although there are countless stories of people who claim to have had near death experiences, no one has ever died and been able to confirm what exactly happens to our spirits after death. Those who have clinically died momentarily having what we call a near death experience, or NDE, do return to the physical bodies recalling similar encounters.

Most NDE cases report an out-of-body experience. Most of them report seeing their lifeless physical body from above. For those who are not immediately revived, they usually describe traveling through a tunnel with a bright light at the end. Many also describe seeing loved ones who had passed before them.

Prior to returning to the physical body, the individual usually experiences a voice or at least some sense of being informed that he must return - it isn't their time to go.

In recent years physiological explanations that have arisen to debunk these experiences as connected with the process of death. In a study that began on heart attack patients in 2006, Dr. Sam Parnia of South Hampton University concluded, "evidence is now suggesting that mental and cognitive processes may continue for a period of time after a death has started". Dr. Parnia calls the experience as "essentially a global stroke of the brain. Therefore like any stroke process, one would not expect the entity of mind/consciousness to be lost immediately". Some researchers believe that the experience could be caused from cerebral anoxia (lack of oxygen to the brain) and secretions from the pineal gland that occur at death causing the brain to continue to function for a brief period of time and certain symptoms, such as a narrowing of vision and seeing a bright light, are merely chemical reactions in the brain. No matter which school of thought one prefers, the end result is still the same. The ultimate mystery of life is death.

Parapsychology

On June 19, 1957, the Parapsychological Association began at Duke University. Parapsychologists set out to scientifically prove that spirits of those who had died continued to exist on another plane. Yet, ghost hunting and proving life after death is only a small part of the modern parapsychology. The scope of practice for the parapsychologist includes NDE, telepathy, precog-nition, clairvoyance, telekinesis, reincarnation, and paranormal phenomena.

The realm of near death experiences includes out of body experiences (OBE) or astral projection. Countless stories have cropped up through the past few decades of living people leaving the physical body and traveling in the "astral body". Some have done this intentionally, spending years training in order to experience travel beyond the confines of a physical body. In many spiritual paths, masters are said to have the ability to leave the physical body and travel on the spiritual plane. It is believed in many occult systems that the astral body connects to the physical by means of a silver cord. The danger of astral projection is that there are discarnate spirits wandering on that plane of existence and it is possible for one to walk in and literally hijack the physical body. Renowned parapsychology pioneer and researcher Swedenborg wrote extensively of his experiences with OBE in "Spiritual Diary," 1747-1765.

ESP or extrasensory perception is described by many sources as "reception of information not gained through the recognized physical senses but sensed with the mind". Often referred to us as our sixth sense, this ability is present in all of us.

Some people have a natural tendency to be more sensitive in that area while others have fine-tuned this ability through meditation and practice. There is nothing magical or supernatural about it. Every living creature possesses this primal sense. Where we humans fall short is by ignoring our "gut feeling" and rationalizing situations because we are taught not to trust our intuition but to think our way through situations. This oftentimes results in wishing we would have trusted our initial feeling and followed our instincts.

One example of ESP is when we know when someone is watching us. We feel their stare. How many times have you sensed that someone was looking at you only to turn around and directly meet his or her gaze? How many times have you walked into a situation where two people were having an argument or disagreement and even though they attempted to hide the bad feelings between them, you sensed that something negative was happening before you appeared on the scene? These are all episodes of ESP. A psychic is merely a person with above average ESP abilities. ESP is broken up into several categories.

Telepathy is the psychic transfer of information from one individual to another. I have a thought and I transfer it, without speaking to another using only my mind. The other person receives the thought and knows what I am thinking. A thought is merely a form of energy so we are talking about the transference of energy.

Psychokinesis, or Telekinesis, is the ability to move a physical object using only the mind. This is easier said than done. I have been able to accomplish this a few times in my life but only under circumstances where I was very emotional and it was unintentional. On one occasion, I was very upset over a situation with a mortgage company during the purchase of a property. As I ranted on the phone over the mistakes that had been made, I had the phone in one hand and was motioning with my other one, as if they could see that. Each time I waved my hand, Christmas cards that were taped to the wall started flying off and hitting the floor. Once I realized what was happening, it stopped abruptly and I was unable to force it.

Psychometry involves receiving information from inanimate objects. This is another difficult activity and not for the novice. I fine-tuned this ability by becoming a Reiki healer. Through my hands, I was attuned to pick up on pain and illness in others and transfer that negative energy out while bringing in healing universal energy to replace it. Unfortunately, this type of fine-tuning in someone like myself, already sensitive to psychic energy, can cause problems. I found that I had become a psychic sponge. I absorbed the energy of everyone I touched. I was getting so sick from putting my hands on clients that I had to stop all forms of touch therapy. Just shaking hands with someone puts me a risk for picking up energy that I don't necessarily want. I also found this to be true in touching certain objects.

Many years ago, I decided to get a palm reading. Before examining my palms, the reader asked me to place my hands palms down on her table. Within seconds, pain shot up my arms like electrical currents. I immediately removed my hands and explained to the reader what I had experienced. She then informed me that the people who had previously put their hands there included someone going through a divorce, someone on the verge of suicide, and someone who recently lost his job. All of the energy from these people remained where their hands had been on that table and I picked up the negative emotions and pain through my own hands. I am very careful these days as to who and what I touch.

Other forms of psychic abilities include clairvoyance, which literally means clear vision. The clairvoyant sees visions which often times appear as a timeline or even as a movie in their mind. The vision can be related to a past or future event. Some clairvoyants see the visions in the form of a prophetic dream.

A clairvoyant is not necessarily a medium although many are. The psychic gift takes many forms. Some with the gift do nothing but see future events, like many psychic readers. Others, who can envision the past, often use their talents to solve cold cases with law enforcement authorities.

Mediums specifically see and/or communicate with spirits of the deceased. Channeling involves the medium becoming possessed and communicating directly as the spirit. This communication can be verbal, or the entranced medium will write what the spirit is communicating: automatic writing.

Parapsychology is most recognized by the general public for its work with the afterlife. We remain ever inquisitive seeking for answers to assure us of some existence after death. This quest propels parapsychology to continue to seek more advanced technology for proof of life after death. The afterlife and the psychic workings of our minds continue to intrigue scientist and occultist alike. The ethereal realm of the soul is the true last frontier.

All Hauntings Are Not Created Equal

Television shows the extreme in what we consider to be a haunting. These shows are based on sensationalism and communication with active, intelligent entities. I always found it interesting that these shows have such accuracy with finding active hauntings. This is hardly reality. The vast majority of hauntings are residual; there is no intelligent entity present but rather an energetic impression left in an area. The haunting repeats itself again and again very much like a tape or video playing in a loop. The causes of residual hauntings can anything from a trauma or strong emotion to a repetitive action such as a shutter slamming over and over again. These types of hauntings cannot be photographed, or videotaped, and they do not respond to communication.

Residual hauntings are commonly experienced as smells. This holds true particularly in instances where there was once a fire involved. Often the smell of smoke or burnt material can be experienced in such an area. Sounds are also prevalent as in cases where voices or music can still be heard.

Most residual hauntings are so subtle that in the normal course of daily activity, they would go unnoticed. Most residuals are not noticed until the quieter times, such as late at night or the early morning hours when other daily noises are not present. This is why many people believe that hauntings occur at only certain hours.

In reality, it is during these hours that such subtleties would be noticed. Because residuals are so inconspicuous, it is easy for the conscious mind to rationalize away their very existence.

Residual emotions and trauma left in a location can be extremely powerful. A good example of this sort of energy can be found in Club 1135 on Decatur Street in the French Quarter. That entire block of Decatur is directly behind the Ursuline Convent, the oldest building in the Mississippi Valley. Those buildings currently occupying that block were used for over 200 years as hospital facilities and housing for nurses. 1135 Decatur Street had been used specifically for yellow fever patients.

During an investigation of the building, investigators experienced nausea and a sensation of feeling feverish as they attempted to gather evidence throughout the building. Some had become so sick that they had to leave the premises. In heavy residuals, it is common to feel emotions, sickness, sensations of hot and cold, and smells associated with the location.

Hospitals and mental asylums are notorious for residual hauntings, as are battlefields and prisons.

A few years ago, I spent a weekend in Vicksburg, which is surrounded by the battlefield. Before checking into my hotel, I drove around the area just to get accustomed to my surroundings. I wound up getting a lot more than I bargained for. Within minutes I saw flashing images of war; cannons firing, heavy smoke, and horses trampling throughout. I caught glimpses of young men firing at one another, others lying on the ground bleeding, some were dead. The images were so intense that I was unable to visit the battlefield later on my trip. I felt so drained from just driving around the area that I feared I might become physically sick if I continued. I spent the entire weekend resting in my room. When I checked out, I quickly hit the highway and got out of Vicksburg.

I had a similar experience in Angola State Penitentiary several years earlier. One of the prison executives had taken one of my tours and invited me to the prison rodeo. When I arrived she had arranged for me to have a private tour of the prison facility. Angola is the largest maximum-security penitentiary in the country. It is often called the Alcatraz of the South. The 18,000-acre prison is surrounded on three sides by the Mississippi River. The fourth side is separated from freedom by a large alligator infested moat. Part of my visit included both the old execution room, which included an antiquated electric chair (Old Sparky) and the current execution room where lethal injections are administered. In both places the energy in the rooms felt very heavy, it was difficult to breathe. I became overcome with the putrid smell of death. There was a foreboding feeling the entire time I was in both buildings.

The active or intelligent haunting is best described as a disembodied spirit of someone who was once human. We as humans have several layers to our bodies. We have a physical body, but also an astral body, an ethereal body and a spirit body. All of our bodies are comprised of energy. This energy extends from our bodies as far as seventeen feet.

Kirlian photography has enabled us to actually photograph that energy or *aura* that extends from us. The true self is not merely the physical. Energy cannot be destroyed, only changed. When the physical body dies, the energy within leaves its shell and continues to live in another state outside of what is physical reality.

For the most part, active hauntings are seen in the peripheral vision. This is probably due to the fact that peripheral vision easily captures motion. The slightest flicker of movement is easily detected. Often times, an individual will catch a glimpse of a ghost out of the corner of his eye, then look straight on and see nothing. It is easy to rationalize the vision away in most cases. Many people assume that they are "seeing things" when in fact they have witnessed a ghost.

I have spoken to numerous people through the years who had seen full-bodied apparitions right before their eyes. Some people have even had conversations with such with no idea that it is a ghost. Some spirits have, on occasion, appeared and spoken to an individual then disappeared. Oddly enough, often times, this occurs with individuals who are not looking for ghosts. Unfortunately, during paranormal investigations, full-bodied apparitions do not appear nor do they readily start conversations.

Spirits have the ability to materialize and dematerialize on our physical plane. Without the confines of the physical body, their vibrational rate is much higher than ours. Humans can experience this materialization on the physical plane in number of ways; most commonly by feeling sensations rather than actually seeing something.

Haunting can be attached to places, people, or even objects. There are numerous cases of "haunted" antiques that are purchased from estate sales or individuals receiving a piece of furniture that belonged to a loved one only to have the loved one still attached to it. A mirror in the Hollywood Roosevelt Hotel is said to be haunted by the ghost of Marilyn Monroe. Once located in the Cabana Suite 229, a maid cleaning the room claimed to see the reflection of a young, blonde woman standing behind her. When she turned, no one was there. Only when she looked into the mirror again would she return. Others began to make similar claims. The hotel eventually moved the mirror to a more public location and placed with it a photograph of Marilyn.

A common theme in haunted objects is haunted dolls or toys. One of the most terrifying of such is

Annabelle, a giant Raggedy Ann doll. The doll belonged to a young nurse named Donna in the 1970s. It was intended only as decoration and Donna placed the doll every day on her freshly made bed. But soon she began to notice that the doll moved on her own. Donna would return home from work and find the doll had changed positions. Not only did Annabelle change positions, she also changed rooms.

Donna and her roommate, Angie, would find little notes left around the apartment. The notes simply said "Help Lou," and "Help us." They appeared to have been written by a child. The young women became curious and contacted a medium who conducted a séance in the apartment. The medium made contact with the spirit who claimed to be that of a seven-year-old girl named Annabelle Higgins who had died on the property many years before. Annabelle explained that all she could do was move the doll to get their attention. The child asked if she could live inside the doll. The women agreed to allow it. That's when the situation took a terrifying turn for the worse.

Annabelle began physically attacking a friend of Angie's, Lou. Lou had strange dreams about the doll trying to strangle him. At some point, he even awakened with claw marks and scratches on his chest and stomach. Oddly, Annabelle had dried blood on her clothing and hands. The trio called an Episcopal priest to the home in an attempt to rid themselves of the spirit. When an exorcism failed to solve the problem, paranormal investigators Ed and Lorraine Warren were called in. They removed the doll from the premises to study.

The Warrens were convinced that it was a demonic spirit that used the doll to manipulate the girls and Lou. They believed that its next step was to possess one of them. They convinced the girls to allow them to take Annabelle away. On their trip home with Annabelle, the Warrens experienced episodes of the car jerking then eventually stalling. Ed took a vial of holy water and made the sign of the cross as he sprinkled it over Annabelle. This seemed to calm down the situation until they could get home.

Ed placed Annabelle on a chair in his office. Over the next several days, the doll began moving about the house. Although no one in the Warren home was attacked, they opted to put the evil doll in a glass encasement in their occult museum, where she remains today. Visitors report Annabelle moving and changing positions inside her case. Some even report hearing her growl. One visitor made the mistake of challenging her to "do something" to him if she was able to. When he left the museum on his motorcycle, he lost control hitting a tree. He was killed instantly.

Ghostly attachments to people are very common. A woman sent some photos of her wedding to me. In each photo there was a presence visible. She immediately assumed that the location where the wedding was held was haunted. After reviewing all of her photos, it became apparent that the spirit was attached to her rather than the location. When I suggested this, she confirmed that she had sensed the presence of her grandmother during the ceremony.

A good friend of mine, Gary, contacted me in early spring, 2009, and told me of a strange experience he had had. He said, "I have this weird thing going on. I liked to walk in the cemeteries by Canal Street sometimes, because it was so peaceful. It's where I meditated and could tune into writing my music. But I happened to come upon a very strange gravesite; a ten-year-old boy was buried there in 1924. I need you to go check it out, the headstone read, 'Mother, I'm going to play.'"

He told me that when he first saw this, a chill ran down his spine. All he could imagine was that it was the last thing the boy said to his mother before he died. He reached out to touch the boy's tomb. When he placed his hand of the faceplate, he felt a charge like an electrical shock go up his arm. He jerked his arm away quickly. Feeling a bit unnerved from the experience, he went home and stayed away from the cemetery. From that day forward, he received visits from the little boy in his dreams. He often awakened in the middle of the night and would see the boy standing at his bedside, and then he'd disappear. Sometimes even when he was awake, he would see a young boy darting about in his apartment.

"When did this happen?" I asked.

His response shocked me. "About twenty years ago," he stated in a very matter of fact manner.

"Twenty years ago? Seriously? And you're just telling me now?" I shrieked.

"Well, the kid's ghost had stopped for a while but now he's back and I don't know what he wants. I've been seeing him a lot lately. Go to the cemetery and check it out," he instructed.

"Ok, I'll go tomorrow, meet me there," I suggested.

"No. I want you to go check it out. I can't go back in there. I don't ever want to go back in there. I don't want to attract anything else. I have enough problems," he explained.

"Alright, I'll go on my own. You're probably right," I resigned.

The following day, I ventured into the cemetery in search of the gravesite. Gary's directions, after twenty years, were vague and New Orleans cemeteries can be confusing. It was April, gypsy moth caterpillar season. These large stinging caterpillars dwell in moss-covered oak trees, falling onto everything. I am deathly afraid of them. I carefully tiptoed through the tombs watching for caterpillars. They were everywhere. Some of them were over six inches long, wriggling over tombstones and wall vaults. I found the wall vault and quickly took a photo of it with my phone. I catapulted back to my vehicle and got out there.

I delved into the state records and found a death record for the boy. The child had drowned in what was the New Basin Canal, a former waterway that ran from Lake Pontchartrain to the Mississippi River. The odd part was there no obituary for the boy, no funeral notices, and no news article about a drowning boy. We did learn from Gary's father that children commonly drowned in the Canal as many of them dove into it off of barges that traveled the waterway. It seemed very strange that a child that age would tragically drown and the family didn't even announce the death. Yet there was a death certificate and a gravesite.

The strangest part of the incident is that the boy's address was listed on the death record. The address was two doors down from where Gary had lived as a child, until he was ten years old.

The boy had drowned many years before Gary lived on that street so he couldn't have possibly known him. We did find out from the cemetery office that it could have been a case where the child perhaps fell into the canal, but his body never retrieved. He may have later been presumed dead and the family had his name encrypted on the tomb. Tombs in New Orleans are commonly shared by families and often times names added on faceplates even if there was no burial. We pondered over the situation.

"We really don't know that he's even in that vault," I told him.

"I wonder how we could find out…" he replied with an inquisitive look in his eyes.

"I know what you're thinking, and no, we're not going to crack off that faceplate just to see what's in there. It's called grave robbing and we'd never get away with it," I said sarcastically.

"We did all we can do, we have to leave it as we just don't know. We'll never know," I stated.

The mystery of the drowned little boy remains. For whatever reason, he had attached himself to my friend and continued to visit him. Some psychics have suggested a past life connection to the boy. Others think that perhaps the connection of the old address is something familiar to the little spirit. Not all cases are solved with any concrete conclusions. Gary accepted that this spirit had become attached to him. I recounted the story in one of the episodes on Haunted New Orleans. He even included it in one of his songs, "When Angels Look Away." After a while, he quit discussing the ghost with me. I respected that he no longer wanted to dwell on it. I don't know if it ever stopped.

A little over three years after he told me of his ghostly companion, the angels took Gary away. Was there some karmic connection to this spirit? Was the spirit connection some sort of forewarning of my friend's untimely death? Perhaps I'll never know.

Other Unexplained Phenomena

Some types of hauntings have absolutely nothing to do with ghosts or the deceased, as in the case of the poltergeist. Once believed to be an unhappy spirit, today parapsychologists believe that this phenomenon is actually caused by psychic energy of a living person. It is often times uncontrolled energy from an adolescent or mentally disturbed individual. The usual occurrences experienced in poltergeist phenomena include objects thrown across a room or falling off shelves, doors slamming, and objects moving around on their own.

Emotions that are not expressed become stored in the body. These repressed emotions can later manifest themselves in the physical body as pain, disease or emotional disturbances. Sometimes however, rather than storing in the body, the emotional energy gets thrown into the physical plane and can be experienced as what might be perceived as psychic phenomena. This is particularly true in instances where an individual is more psychically sensitive. To the untrained individual it would be a normal reaction to assume that this type of energy disbursement would be coming from an outside source. When in reality, the energy is coming from an internal one. A good example of this type of energy disbursement can be explained best in the case of repressed anger. Anger is a particularly volatile emotion. If anger is not expressed, it turns inward. In individuals who have mastered not being in touch with their emotions and denying them, the anger gets buried deep in the physical body. Many years later, pain and illness manifest caused by the stored emotions. In those who have a hard time controlling their emotions but through guilt or other pressures attempt to push it inward, this anger could very well project itself through other venues. A good example is the passive-aggressive personality and those who are mentally or emotionally ill. There is a certain "energy" that surrounds such individuals that gives a feeling of "something not right" to those around them. Depressed people are often described as having a "black cloud over them." Manic people have a fast paced or racing type of energy around them. This is why "moods" can be contagious. It is the energy that is thrown off from particular individuals and how others receive it. Enthusiastic people send out enthusiastic vibrations that can be felt by others, who in turn begin to feel enthusiastic. Negative people send out negative vibrations that can bring others down or make them feel tired. It is all part of the normal human energetic field. Adolescents throw off huge amounts of energy due to changing hormones in the body. This energy is sometimes projected out of the body and creates movement or disruption in a particular area.

It's always a good idea to make sure that reports of poltergeist activity begin with a thorough interview with the homeowner. If the family includes anyone with mental disturbances, drug or heavy alcohol use, a menopausal woman, or adolescent, then disturbances within the home could be stemming from one of its living inhabitants rather than a ghost.

An entity known as the Doppelganger is considered the fourth type of haunting, but like the poltergeist, not a ghost of someone who has died, but the ethereal double of someone living. The word literally means "double walker." It appears as an exact replica of the person and often times deceives others in thinking that it is the actual person. It will generally appear to be solid from a distance, but tends to act strangely or mechanically. Seeing the double is often the presage of the imminent death of the person. The poet Percy Shelley saw his double shortly before drowning. As did Lady Diana Rich, daughter of the Earl of Holland; she saw her double in a garden a month before she died of smallpox. According to English medium Eileen J. Garrett, the double is a means of telepathic and clairvoyant projection, which can be manipulated to expand one's consciousness.

Another type of entity that is getting recent attention is what some refer to as *shadow people* or *shadow spirits.* It is unsure if these shadow folk are truly ghosts or possibly something else. Some people even insist that they are extraterrestrials. They appear in shadow form only and in the shape of a human. There are no features, however. They are long and thin. Some are reported to have no necks. Whatever they are, it seems that they vanish when as soon as attention is given to them. My first recollection of seeing a spirit as a child was just a shadow. On my investigation of the State Palace Theater, as outlined in my other book, *Tales From The French Quarter*, we happened to capture one on video. We had opened up a closet door and it was seen in the back of the closet. When I entered the closet for a closer look, it vanished.

If the haunting is indeed active and intelligent, the next step is the actual investigation.

The Investigation

There are several angles to the successful investigation; the scientific research and the psychic research. The first step is to research the history of the building to determine who might have died there. This is very simple to do if the area is a historical district, as these areas have documen-tation easily available to the public. For properties not in historical areas it is more difficult, especially if it is a large city. The best place to start is mortgage records. This will give you information of who owned a property and when. This will not give you information on renters in a property. This information may be impossible to obtain. In residential properties, it is sometimes better to interview other people in the neighborhood about a property's history. Historical research can be very tedious. You need to find out who lived in the property and who might have died there, along with any pertinent information with regard to unusual paranormal activity. Usually, property owners or nearby neighbors are somewhat familiar with the history of a property. Never overlook the history of the area prior to the existing building. Oftentimes it is not energy from a recent event but from what occurred in a specific area long before a house or building was on the land. In Louisiana, it is common for entire subdivisions to be built on land that was once a plantation or prior Native American land. Sometimes the energy left in an area can be hundreds of years old. It is important to look at the entire history of not only the building but also the land and surrounding area.

The second step is to check newspaper and police archives. In New Orleans, all of this information is available through the library. It is necessary to check the local newspaper to see where their archives are located and if it is accessible to the public. Do not expect this information to be available on the Internet. The New Orleans archives were a collection of hand written index cards that correlated to microfiche files. The machine was so antiquated that it was turned by hand to go through the film. Old police reports and coroner's records are usually archived on microfiche as well. Going through old records can be as tedious as trying to find a needle in a haystack. When I wrote my first book, I spent three and a half years searching through old files in the New Orleans archives.

It is important that you do your own historical research rather than rely solely on the property owner to provide the information. Even the most honorable homeowners can provide incorrect information that will lead you on a wild goose chase. If information is provided, verify it.

During one investigation I conducted for a television show, I was pressed for time and took the information from the homeowner who seemed to have done her homework. She had originally contacted me claiming that a malevolent spirit of the former owner haunted her home. She informed my team and I that a cult leader who conducted black masses and necromantic rituals at one time owned the home. She told of an evil magician who conducted sexual orgies and animal sacrifices as part of his rituals. She even went so far as to say he lured in young men into his self-made religion for sexual purposes. She told me that the cult leader had died shortly after Katrina and just a month before she had purchased the fully furnished house. She reported that all the mirrors in the house had been covered or painted over, and that her new mirrors were shattering with no physical cause. She also had found human remains under the sub floor of the house when she replaced the floor.

Although she seemed hysterical, I gave her the benefit of the doubt. There are certainly people out there, especially in New Orleans, who practice rituals based on the necromancy magic of Aleister Crowley. Crowley was a high ceremonial magician in the early 1900s that dabbled in rituals, including trying to reanimate the dead. He created several magical orders that have followers to this day. What the homeowner had described sounded very much like something that might be related. So it made sense.

The investigation and psychic investigation both indicated a male spirit in the house. Even the best psychics can be swayed when fed the wrong information. Once information is provided, it is very easy for the mind to create a story about the property. Even if the psychic is unaware of the initial history, if he/she is brought into a situation where people nearby are projecting their thoughts, that misinformation can easily be picked up. The only thing I felt in the house was the presence of a female entity, probably a former caretaker on the second floor and a benevolent male presence that felt as if he had been there for many years. I felt nothing malevolent.

We investigated and filmed the episode. We encouraged the owner to have a cleansing done on the house to remove any residual energy. Shortly thereafter, another network wanted a property that included animals in the haunting. It just so happened that this particular woman had four dogs. I recommended the property to the network.

In just one short month after my visit, when I returned with the new network, the woman reported increased activity. More mirrors had broken. The dogs were even more agitated than before. It seemed as if whatever was in that house was kicked up over the increase in investigations…or so it seemed.

During the filming, the show's resident ghost hunters decided to attempt to communicate with the spirit. I was invited to attend this session. I watched in horror as the celebrity ghost hunters baited this woman, spiraling her more and more into hysteria. The more hysterical she became, the more the ghostly activity increased. The more she reacted, the more they baited her. Finally, I realized what was going on.

This woman lived in the house with her very large family. The more she became unnerved, so did the other members of the house, including the four dogs. All of the psychic energy that was being thrown around by those in the home was creating poltergeist activity. Things were falling off of walls, glass and mirrors broke, and it was a domino effect. I also believed that she had begun to enjoy the attention of a couple television shows.

Towards the end of filming the second show, I happened to run into someone I knew very well and mentioned the property location. Much to my surprise this person knew the former owner. Hardly a Crowley type magician conducting satanic rituals, the man was a Santero, a priest of Santeria. Not only was he nothing like the new owner had portrayed him; he wasn't even dead! The man was elderly and had become quite ill. He had spent the past several years in a nursing home in a coma. None of the information provided by this new home owner was true. I felt like a complete idiot and totally betrayed by the homeowner. I'll never know if she was just driven by fear or if she intentionally created this situation to get herself on television. It hardly matters. At the end of the day, I have only myself to blame for not properly researching the history on my own. It was a valuable lesson learned.

Once you have researched the history of the property and gotten preliminary information on the activity from the residents, it is time to move on to the actual investigation. The scientific equipment needed for an investigation is easily found on the Internet and anyone can purchase it. The first is the electro-magnetic meter. The use of electro-magnetic meters measure energy in particular areas that might be considered haunted. They are used to seek out disruptions in the natural magnetic field of locations. Unseen on our physical plane, the spirit plane is parallel to the physical. Those who are particularly sensitive to psychic energy can often feel the energy in this parallel dimension. Sensitive meters specifically designed to detect the electro-magnetic currency of such energy can measure this energy.

EMF meters can be purchased at prices ranging from under one hundred dollars up. It really depends on how elaborate you want to be. The less expensive ones usually have a needle to gage the readings whereas the more expensive ones often are digital. I personally rely more on my psychic attunement and merely use meters to back it up. The main purpose for me to use the meters was when I was initially researching the hauntings for the tours. We were selling tours as "actual documented hauntings" and I wanted to make sure that they were properly documented. In my work, I use photography and video equipment that give me more validity. Meter readings alone are not enough to create evidence of spirit activity. It is however a very good back up for looking for paranormal activity.

Meter readings are only a small part of the investigation. I believe that they are an important part of a successful investigation but I work more on the spiritual and psychic end of the spectrum; therefore, do not rely on them as other investigators might.

Readings can be produced by something other than the supernatural. Always make sure that you are not reading a person in the next room. These devices are very sensitive and can pick up readings through walls.

Motion detectors are also sometimes used in investigations. There are so many variables present with motion detectors that I have never bothered with one. Additionally, having had motion detectors in my home for so many years, I believe that if spirits would set them off, mine would have gone off by now. I work extensively with not only ghosts but also other spirits and have never had an incident where the alarm went off spontaneously. I do not consider motion detectors to be a sufficient means of detecting paranormal activity.

Changes in temperature are also a common factor when spirits are present. This is due to the change in the energetic frequency of spirit manifesting on the physical plane.

Shifts in atmospheric temperature occur when energy is shifted between planes. The uses of non-contact thermometers are used to measure changes in atmospheric temperatures when spirits are present. As with the meters, these can be purchased rather inexpensively. The thermometer is helpful in locating active areas by detecting subtle temperature changes. Non-contact thermometers are also sometimes called thermal scanners.

Many years ago I conducted the investigation at the Myrtles Plantation, America's most haunted house. There are numerous active hauntings at the Myrtles. General David Bradford built it in 1796 on land that the indigenous natives used as sacred burial ground. He not only killed the Native Americans on the property, but also dug up already buried Natives and burned their remains on the property. Unaware of the "curse" associated with the land, General Bradford willed the property to his daughter, Sarah Mathilde. Sarah Mathilde married Judge Clark Woodruff and had two daughters with him. The family had a slave woman who cared for the children named Chloe. It is suspected that Chloe was also a mistress to Judge Woodruff. One evening, the judge caught Chloe eavesdropping on an argument he was having with his wife. In an attempt to punish her, he cut off her left ear. From that day forward, she wore a tignon (head wrap) on her head to conceal the disfigurement.

Shortly thereafter, one of the Woodruff daughters celebrated a birthday and Chloe was asked to bake a cake. Chloe added poisonous oleander leaves to cake in an attempt to make Sarah and the girls ill. Some believed it to be an act of vengeance, others an attempt to regain the family's trust by nursing them back to health. The plan backfired. Sarah Mathilde and both girls died. Fearing retribution themselves from the grieving Judge Woodruff, the other slaves lynched Chloe from one of the oak trees that lined the property.

Judge Woodruff later sold the property to the Sterling family who also had a daughter named Sarah. Two of the male children had died while living on the property. Sarah Sterling eventually inherited the home from her parents. She married an attorney, William Winter, and had two sons and a daughter whom were raised on the Myrtles Plantation. Like many children in the 1800s, the little girl became ill with yellow fever during one of the many epidemics that plagued Louisiana. When doctors were unable to successfully cure the child's illness, the Winters' brought to their home a Voodoo Priestess named Cleo to heal her. Cleo's efforts were fruitless; the young girl died. Blamed for her death, Cleo was hung that same night from the chandelier in the ladies parlor.

In 1871, William Winter was sitting in his parlor reading to his sons, when he heard a carriage pull up outside. He then heard a man's voice yell out, "I am here to see the attorney." When William Winter opened the front door, an unknown assailant with a shotgun killed him. Mortally wounded, he dragged his bleeding body up the stairs of his home. He made it to the 17th step where he fell into Sarah's arms and died.

On this property, the thermometer became an invaluable tool in my investigation. One of the main parlor areas was significantly colder than that of the rest of the house. This temperature variance was picked up not only by the thermometer but by our bodies as well. The first thing I checked was the central air system. The cold room was not on a separate system. The air coming out of all of the vents measured the same temperature consistently throughout the plantation. Yet, in the one room, a thin layer of frost covered the windows. We knew that this was the most active area of the house. During filming, the thermometer changed rapidly ranging from the upper 69 degrees falling down into the lower 50s and back. It is impossible for such changes to occur so rapidly in one space, so we had to conclude that it was spiritual activity creating the changes in temperature. Many researchers believe that spirits utilize energy (heat) in order to manifest on the physical plane. As the spirit draws existing heat in an area, a cold spot is produced. The meters didn't really give us any significant readings in the room so this is why the meters alone are inadequate. Obviously thermometers do not work outdoors or in unheated buildings when the weather is cold. For outdoors, some investigators use a relative humidity gauge. It records the ambient conditions of an outdoor location. Some investigators find these helpful in ruling out natural effects that may appear in photos.

Changes in readings should be quite obvious. You don't have to take a course or be a rocket scientist to use any of the tools for investigations. None of the above mentioned devices are infallible either. There have been many times that I got nothing on meters and had activity show up in photographs or on video. You always have to remember that this is not an exact science. It is for this reason that it is important to use a variety of equipment as well as the use of psychics that will be discussed in future chapters. It is a combination of many different tools that is used in determining haunted activity. You should never rely on any one source to make conclusive decisions about an investigation.

Other devices that are used in paranormal investigations are the Geiger counter and the ion particle counter. The Geiger counter is used to monitor changes in radiation levels that are believed to be present during ghost activity. The ion particle counter measures particles in the air and changes in them that might occur in the presence of paranormal activity. This is particularly useful in checking for density in anomalies. I have even heard of some investigators using something as simple as a compass. The compass needle is said to spin out of control in the presence of paranormal activity.

It should be pointed out at this time that even if you get readings on all of the equipment mentioned here, it does not necessarily mean that an area is haunted per se. As I mentioned in the previous chapter, there are many, many spiritual beings on the other side. It is important to go beyond the use of scientific equipment to determine if the energy in a specific location is indeed a ghost. There are many paranormal investigators who rely solely on scientific measures to determine activity. If, for instance, there is an elemental (low vibrational spirit) present, you will get readings on your equipment. Elementals have no defined personality. They are spirit by definition but not a ghost of someone who once lived. If you use any of the mentioned devices in areas of energy vortices or portals, you will see variances in readings. In fact, when there is a presence of higher vibrational spirits in an area, the readings will be quite strong. Many people during the Bell Witch experience, discussed in detail in a later chapter, got phenomena in equipment readings as well as photographs but it did not prove that the entity was the spirit of someone who was once alive. In the case of residual hauntings, it might not be impossible to obtain any evidence. Lack of evidence does not necessarily indicate the lack of a haunting.

One of the most valuable tools used in investigations that I have found is the digital audio recorder. These pick up *electronic voice phenomena* or EVP. As with any other equipment, there are a wide variety of brands, types, and prices when it comes to digital recorders. Most digital recorders will plug directly into the computer making downloading audio files relatively simple. Some paranormal investigators use tape recorders to get voice phenomena. I have never had very much luck using tape. I make a point to experiment with different tools. I keep what works and readily discard what does not. If you find that using tape works best for you, then use it.

Digital is much more sensitive and I have had much better results with it. The rule of thumb is "whatever works". Digital recorders are extremely sensitive and will pick up every background sound. It is important when you are trying to get EVP to keep talking and background sound down to minimum. When you first set the recorder, which should be voice activated, it is good to do some talking to establish normal human voices. I generally set up a recorder in a room and leave it. This is to insure that the sounds you are getting are in fact spirit voices.

Note that voices from the spirit plane do not sound like our voices. Often times it sounds like whispering or even growling. I have found the best way to decipher what is on a digital recorder is to play it back, then again in slow motion. When I first began to use the recorder, I got nothing more than a bunch of growling and mumbling. When I slowed the playback down, I found that I was able to understand the "voice" from the other side. On one of my earliest experiences with EVP, I tested it on one of the rooms in my own home that seemed to have more activity than others. I had a house-guest at the time. Katherine Ramsland was in the process of writing her book "*Ghosts!*" and was staying with me to do investigations. She happened to be occupying the bedroom where some strange phenomena had been occurring. Earlier that year, I had another friend staying in the room while visiting and he reported seeing a shadowy apparition appear on the ceiling of the room and then disappear. Other guests had similar experiences while visiting and sleeping in that room. We purchased a small digital recorder and set it to record while she slept in the room. The results, at first, were rather frightening.

In one of the recordings, there was a specific male voice that seemed to be yelling, "Get out!" Katherine had been working with a malevolent spirit and feared that he was warning her. When I later slowed down the playback of the voice, I found that he wasn't saying, "get out," but "let me out." In between his yelling, there was whispering of many voices. The male voice would intermittently yell, "No!" I got the impression that this was possibly a spirit new to the other side and was perhaps just realizing that he was no longer living.

Some newly deceased spirits do not realize immediately that they have died. This is a common theme in many cases with intelligent hauntings. Often the death was untimely and the spirit experienced shock and denial. As hard as it may seem, it is best to leave those spirits alone to accept their reality when they are ready. Trying to convince such a spirit to accept their death will only result in causing more stress and hysteria in the spirit. Communication with such an entity should be short and gentle, and allow that spirit to work through their trauma on their own.

Throughout the many years that I have conducted investigations, I have experienced numerous fascinating EVP recordings. On one investigation, I recorded the voice of a female entity that told me she hated me! During my investigation of the Myrtles Plantation, my group left a digital recorder in the "cold room" while we napped upstairs in preparation for a late night of investigating. When we checked the recorder, we heard the sound of footsteps and a woman's scream. Perhaps it was the sound of William Winter as he made his final ascent up to the seventh stair and into Sarah's arms where he died.

New gadgets such as ghost boxes and talking boxes have emerged over the last few years. I have tried two types and was not impressed by either of them. The Ovilus is a device that gives certain verbal messages in haunted locations. The problem is that it is programmed with various words and it just blurbs them out randomly. Sometimes it will invariably say something that we believe applies to a location. It's all hit and miss, although I have had some strange words come out of it that actually applied to the location I was investigating. When I conducted an investigation of the Banana Courtyard Bed & Breakfast, a former brothel then later a funeral home, the words "funeral" and "grave" did come out of the box. They were mixed in with other random words that did not apply. It is an interesting gadget but I'm not convinced completely of its accuracy.

The most ridiculous new device I've tried is the ghost box. The box is a cheap AM transistor radio that has been hacked to jump channels. Of course you'll hear words from time to time. You'll also hear bits of music. The radio jumps rapidly from channel to channel and again, it is the power of our minds that put the words together and make them mean something relative to the situation. Don't waste your money on these devices.

Regardless of what equipment a person chooses to use in investigations, most importantly always have a supply of fresh batteries on hand to replenish in your equipment. One of the most common mishaps on an investigation is having the energy present drain the batteries in your cameras and equipment. I keep a supply of new different sized batteries in my bag at all times just in case.

There are other things to remember while searching for spirits. Always wear comfortable clothing. If you feel more comfortable, they will feel more comfortable. It is best to wear soft-soled shoes, as well. The less noise you make walking around, the better. Digital devices are very sensitive and it is easy to pick up the sounds of your crew walking around and mistake them for EVP. Choose a location that you know is haunted; this will avoid wild goose chases. Whenever possible, interview property owners and tenants of haunted locations and get some input on what is being experienced. It is best to do a preliminary investigation to obtain data and particulars prior to setting up equipment. Find out if there are certain specifics such as timing involved with the activity. If the ghost is most active at 11 PM, it is silly to begin the investigation at noon. Try to arrange investigations to fall closer to full or new moons. Activity is higher during this time; you won't have much luck if the moon is dark, the 3 days prior to a new moon. Talk to the ghosts when you are there. Acknowledge their presence and tell them why you are there. Never yell or curse at the spirits. It's also a good idea to ask permission to work with it and photograph it. Always have a notebook and pen or a reliable recorder to make notes. Do not depend on your memory for keeping track of data. Keep an open mind and use all of your senses while in a haunted location.

One of the most important things to remember is to never drink or use drugs when dealing with spirits. Aside from the obvious liability of getting hurt on someone's property fumbling around in the dark under the influence, or making mistakes with evidence, it attracts negative entities.

Alcohol and recreational drugs have an effect on brain functioning. The rational mind is in an altered state and the right brain, the psychic side becomes an open channel. Any type of brain altering substance or state can be dangerous when working with the dead. Disembodied spirits that choose to remain attached to the physical plane seek refuse in the bodies of living people who are open. A spirit can literally walk in and possess the body of the living person. Often these types of destructive spirits are attached to the physical because of an addition, drugs or alcohol. They can adversely affect the living by pushing them further into substance abuse and addiction, as mentioned in another chapter. This is why it is extremely important to always be in a fully awake state of awareness at all times when doing an investigation. Prior to stepping into a haunted location, I always pray and meditate to ground and protect myself from such an attachment. Afterwards, I always ground any energy; visualize the energy going into the earth. I also regularly cleanse myself with herbal baths to pull off negative energy from others, living and dead.

Spirit Photography

Among the many devices that are used to prove such existence, one of the most compelling forms of evidence can be examined is what is called spirit photography. Entities can materialize in photographs in many different forms. It is believed that there are certain stages that a spirit will materialize on the physical plane. There is no wrong or right way to capture ghosts on photographs. No one really knows what determines whether or not you will accomplish this. There are no rules, no guidelines. It is unknown whether these entities have the ability to appear on photos at will. We do know that, quite often, equipment failure is a common problem in haunted areas. It is presumed that ghosts do have the ability to control certain situations. Some of the early photographs of ghosts depicted full-bodied apparitions who appeared as transparent people.

With today's advanced photography equipment, we rarely capture such phenomena. One can only surmise that what was passed off as ghostly images in the early 20th century was more likely double exposures rather than actual spirits.

One of the most common forms that can be seen on photographs is called *orbs*. Orbs are seen as spheres of light. They can appear translucent, almost bubble like or have density and color. It is believed that this phase represents the spirit in a condensed form. It is in this manifestation that the spirit travels. Orbs captured on video appear as tiny spheres of light dancing about. They move lightning fast, appearing and disappearing faster than the human eye can see them.

There was one thing that I found very strange with one particular orb photo. The orb was not transparent but very dense and multi-colored. The magnified orb resembled a cell under a microscope. It is interesting to think that possibly the physical body is merely a duplication of the same composite of the spirit. Those who believe in reincarnation, support the theory that the cells with all its DNA and memories are carried from one life to another. The orb in its magnification would seem to support this theory.

There is a lot of controversy over orbs. Orbs have surfaced recently with the invention of digital photography. Orbs have been captured on digital video and have been proven to move in unnatural pattern ruling out dust particles. Sensitive digital equipment can often pick up the minutest particle and it could seem to be something paranormal. You must be able to rule out all physical causes when determining what an orb really is. This can be very difficult to prove. The only case in favor of orbs is that some people have seen glowing balls of light with the naked eye.

The second phase of materialization would be seen as *vortices*. There are several schools of thought of what comprises a vortex. Many believe that the vortex is several orbs traveling together creating the spiral like effect. Other theories include that this is a single spirit in motion. The film literally stops the action on the orb, which is moving in a spiral motion at a very fast speed. If the last theory were correct, then the vortex would actually be the first stage of manifestation on the physical plane, or at least an equal phase.

Once the spirit has settled out of motion, the *ectoplasm*, physical spirit matter, begins to spread much like a fog or mist. This material can also be seen as a string like substance that resembles the vortex. Atmospheric conditions probably have a lot to do with whether the material is seen as dense or sparse. A woman visiting New Orleans several years ago brought a photograph to me that she had taken at Old N'awlins Cookery. In the first frame, a vortex appeared directly over the alligator in the photo. The following shot showed a white fog dispersing over the same area.

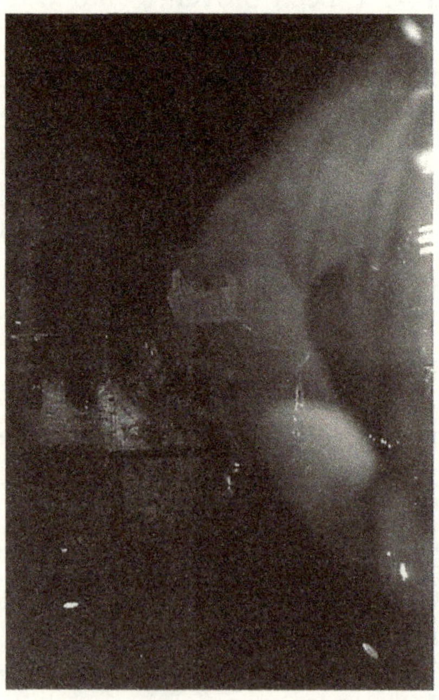

Lastly, and the least common, is the appearance of an *apparition*. An apparition is the appearance of a spirit where actual features appear. An apparition can be of an animal or human. Where it differs from all other forms of spirit is that some sort of identity can made from the form.

Simulacra a term used to describe what appears to be faces or images in almost any kind of inanimate object. A good example of simulacra is seeing images in clouds. It is easy to pick up this sort of thing on old buildings or, as in this case, an old tomb. These sorts of images can be found in almost anything, bricks, wood, textures, & doors. They are optical illusions. Always assume there is a logical explanation for the abnormality until you have ruled out all possibilities. I often get photos sent to me with "faces in windows" that are merely reflections of something else seeming to have the form of a face or partial body of an entity. This is not to say that it is impossible but it is safe to say that usually the images are due to simulacra.

Many of these photos captured ghosts using nothing more than a disposable camera. It is a myth that special cameras are needed to capture spirits on film. You can use just about any camera and get results. Some investigators swear by digital cameras. These seem to prove best suited for getting orbs but not ectoplasm. Some even rely on Polaroid although I have never had any results using an instant photo.

When I first began to do investigations, I went to great lengths to capture ghosts on film. I spent hundreds of dollars on expensive infrared film. Infrared film is not only pricey but also very sensitive. It has to be kept refrigerated and can only be handled in total darkness. I bought the top dollar equipment and spent hours waiting to "get something". I made some interesting observations.

There were no guarantees. While I was spending tons of money on film and processing to get maybe one ghost here and there, the average tourist captured much more on disposable cameras. Secondly, they were getting the shots "accidentally". And lastly, if I was going to get a ghost on a photograph, it was going to happen in the first few moments of entering the area, not hours later. There are never guarantees that a ghost is going to appear in any photograph.

Some of the best shots I have seen were taken randomly and without the intent of capturing ghosts on film. There are things you can do to help make it more likely to get that perfect picture. When going to a haunted location, try to take your photos as quickly as possible. It is believed that most spirits are going to "show themselves" in the first several minutes of a newcomer entering its environment.

Many spirits are believed to be quite curious and initially enjoy the attention. They do tend to bore easily and move on rather quickly. There is no need to hang out for hours trying to get a shot. Make sure that your camera lens is clean and free from debris that might be mistaken for phenomena. What is known is that you have a much better chance of getting a ghost in your shot if you shoot photos with people in them. It is far more likely that a spirit will hover around an individual rather than an object in a distance.

Locations where other ghost photos were taken are usually more active areas. If ten other people got a ghost in their photo at a particular location, it is more likely that you will too. A vast majority of ghosts on photos can be chalked up to nothing more than luck. Some people just happen to be in the right place at the right time. Just as some people are more sensitive to psychic activity, some tend to attract spirits more readily than others. I call these people ghost magnets. It is usually people who are more sensitive or more psychic than average. Often children, who are much more sensitive to this sort of activity, will attract spirits into their photos. One explanation can be that many times loved ones who have passed will remain attached to children and want to be near them.

Humid, dense air seems to be more conducive to the spirit forming on the physical plane than thin, dry air. Rainy days are great, but take care that there is not rain on your lens. Rain, sleet or snow can smear on the lens and give the appearance that there is an anomaly present. Rain and other precipitation appear on photographs and are often times mistaken for orbs. Humidity can create condensation on the lens as well.

Glare from direct sunlight, particularly with digital cameras can sometimes give the same look. Always make sure that there is no smoke present that might get in the shot and appear to be ectoplasm.

Dust, pollen and other airborne particles can appear on the photo as well and appear to be orbs.

It is a myth that ghosts appear in photos only taken in complete darkness. Many a photo has been sent to me that was taken in daylight as well as in buildings with full lighting. The use of fast film does seem to work best. If you do shoots in total darkness, you must have a high-powered flash otherwise your photos will turn out black. Be aware that certain objects can fall across the lens and give the appearance of an anomaly. These include camera straps, hair, and fingers. These are often mistaken for vortices. Vortices are transparent to some degree and form circular patterns. Camera straps bend and are not transparent. Hair is seen as partially transparent but lacks the circular patterning.

In addition to still shots, video cameras have become great tools to use in investigations. The best video camera I have found for investigations is the digital 8 camcorder by Sony. It has built in night vision that allows filming in total darkness. Some models come with an option to slow the shutter down giving an even greater infrared range. I have used the camcorder hand held and also on tripod, leaving it alone in certain areas or rooms of a location. I try to have as many camcorders as possible with night shot on investigations. Here is where working with a group comes in handy. You never know where or when something is going to happen or appear. On most investigations I have several people who are in different areas using camcorders and different pieces of equipment.

The important thing to remember with equipment is to use what works best for you. There is no right or wrong way when it comes to selecting what tools are best; it all boils down to personal preference.

It's easy to see how confusing this might get. It takes a lot of experience with photography and a trained eye to distinguish what is a spirit captured on film and what is not.

Many factors can create illusions on photographs. So when attempting to capture ghosts in photos, there are several things to take into consideration.

Here is a quick checklist of what to keep in mind:

- Always make sure your lens in clean and free of scratches.
- Thoroughly wipe the lens if it is a hot or humid day, keeping it free of precipitation.
- Know that rain, snow, and sleet will show on photographs.
- Keep an open mind but always remain conservative.
- Assume there is a logical explanation for the abnormality until you have ruled out all possibilities.
- Take into consideration lighting and film speed. Many people go for shooting in total darkness, knowing that the flash is going to have an effect and may cause something to look like something else.

The Psychic Connection

One of the most important aspects of the paranormal investigation is the psychic side. Many a ghost-hunter relies solely on scientific means to conclude an investigation. I think those who shun the psychic aspect are robbing themselves of half the experience.

It baffles me that many "experts" in the field of paranormal phenomena refuse to give credibility to psychics in investigations. This is like acknowledging light from a lamp but refusing to accept the electricity that powers it. It is this sort of narrow-minded thought pattern that separates the true parapsychologist from the amateur ghost hunter. When choosing a group, it is important to get involved with groups who conduct both scientific and psychic investigations.

Parapsychology covers a large spectrum of phenomena, ghosts being only a part of it. Much of the study of parapsychology is based on ESP.

Some people become psychic later in life after experiencing a near death experience. Coming close to the afterworld somehow opens them up to that other side because they were almost there. This doesn't take away from the people who were always more sensitive in that area but it does seem to amplify it somewhat. Many people who became psychic later in life reported that their abilities came to them after a serious accident or illness in which they came close to death. This is also the case with psychics who have the ability to heal as well.

Generally when I do investigations, I try to have at least one other person present who is psychic to cross reference what is happening. If both people are seeing the same thing at the same time, then it gives the investigation more credibility. I only use other psychics that I have worked with over extended periods of time on investigations. This insures that I am getting the most accurate information possible. Two psychics can literally act as "jumper cables" for the energy and bounce it off one another. Both psychics will get the same exact image at the same exact time. I have worked with some psychics who picked up complementary vibes to mine; as I am empathetic, the other is clairvoyant.

Raquel Digati of the Cape and Islands Paranormal Study Group is one such psychic that complements my channeling during investigations. She and I became friends while she wrote an article about some of my investigations. As it turned out, she had a great interest in the paranormal and was a natural psychic. She asked me to take her to a few of the most active places in New Orleans. I took her to Holt Cemetery, a final resting place for indigents and the only one in New Orleans that buried beneath the ground with no concrete slab to weight down the coffins. It was a frequent location where local magic practitioners conducted rituals. Cemeteries fascinated Raquel. She also belonged to a group in her home of Rhode Island that was dedicated to the preservation of tombs and cemeteries, so this was right up her alley. We spent several minutes walking around while she photographed different gravesites. When we were finished, we headed to the entrance of Holt where we noticed a strange phenomenon. In an area where there was no grave, words appeared in the dirt as if they were being written from beneath the ground. The words "help me" appeared. Raquel took several photographs of the vacant space. I decided to stand on top of the words.

Immediately, I began to get a vision of a large man with a mask or some other cover over his face. He was grabbing me by the neck. My feet felt as if they were lifted off the ground. Only in this vision, I was not myself, experiencing what someone else had a long time ago. I was experiencing the phenomena on not only a clairvoyant but empathetic level.

The woman I was seeing and feeling was small-framed and dark haired. She wore summer clothing that seemed to depict the 1970s. She wore sandals on her feet, shorts and a red halter-top. Her dark hair fell upon her shoulders as she struggled to free herself from the man who had her by the throat. She mumbled something in Spanish as she took her last breath.

After we left the cemetery, it was a couple hours before I could accurately retell what I had experienced. During the experience, I couldn't speak. I felt weak and had no voice for quite a while afterwards.

As we drove back to the French Quarter, I tried to convey to Raquel what I had experienced but couldn't speak. She literally tuned into me psychic and telepathically took the information and then told it back to me as I nodded.

Once I had grounded myself and was "back in my body", Raquel and I were able to make sense of what I had seen and felt. Apparently, this young woman was killed by the man and buried in an unmarked grave in Holt cemetery. Because the cemetery is below the ground, it is constantly being filled in with new dirt. If one were going to hide a body probably the last place someone would think to look is in a cemetery. When I began to interpret what I had seen, I realized that this woman was a prostitute. I saw images of her standing on Tulane Avenue and a car stopping then seeing her getting inside the car. Once inside, she was taken into the darkened Holt where she was raped and strangled to death. There was no way to verify this information, as there are so many crimes in New Orleans that never make the headlines. With no dates or names, it was nearly impossible to conclude what I had experienced by normal means. But I knew what I saw.

Raquel took digital photographs of the words in the soil during our visit to Holt. Oddly enough, even though we both saw the words appear on the ground, the photos showed only dirt. This is an example of a situation where there can be no scientific or historical documentation to back up the phenomena, yet, I cannot forget the strong images that haunt my mind still to this day of this woman struggling with her last breath to free herself from her murderer.

This is Raquel's account of the Holt Cemetery incident as in her report for Cape and Islands Paranormal Research Society:

"I love Holt Cemetery. In New England, the various styles of funerary elegance have skipped the simplicity and eerie nature of Holt. The unmarked graves, the wooden markers, and the obvious poverty that required persons to bury their dead in the manner that was presented intrigued me.

Over what have now become several years of friendship, I have had the pleasure of seeing more than just the 'regular sights' of the incredible city of New Orleans through the grace of Kalila Smith and I am forever grateful.

This cemetery remains as one of those places that nearly defy description. In general one got an impression of sadness, despair, an odd reverence and a glimpse at a culture that would normally be hidden save for the ritualism revealed with how a completely different culture, outside of those wealthy enough to build stylish tombs in the cities more famous areas, reveres their dead.

A most intriguing event occurred; in a blank area of dirt I distinctly saw the words 'Help me' scratched into the dirt. At first I wasn't overly concerned, deciding it was most likely someone with a more morbid sense of humor than I have (if indeed that's possible) enjoying a strange prank. However, I looked closer. The scratches were RAISED, not indented, as if they had been made from beneath the ground. Instant dread slapped me like wet wind and I called out to Kalila who was at another nearby site.

Kalila and I stared at the marks. We tried to recreate the grooves with a stick. We couldn't do it. We tried to photograph the message it would not show up on the film. However, we both sensed that there was more to this than met the eye. So we went with our third eyes.

Over a series of short odd exchanges we concurred that we sensed something amiss in the way of an unmarked grave. Not unmarked due to lack of funds for a stone or cross, but unmarked on purpose. As we attuned ourselves to the situation, we both felt many things but in common we felt the alleged victim of foul play met a nasty end and may have been 'dumped' at that site, and more than a few years ago. Everything beautiful has a dark side, and perhaps this might be an indicator of the possibility of a seedier more frightening side of the otherwise enchanting city of New Orleans."

Nora Natale of Spiritual Magick is another psychic that I have used on investigations. Unlike Raquel complimenting and bouncing off of my connections, Nora is right in line with mine. She will experience exactly what I do at the precise moment. There have been numerous investigations where we had walked into a room and felt and saw the same image. Most psychics will connect easily with one another. And most of the time will have no trouble communicating without words once they get the "bounce" going. This of course can be confusing to the non-psychics in the group who can't quite grasp the non-conversation going on between the psychics. Needless to say, this can be quite amusing for the psychics.

One thing that every psychic and sensitive has to be aware of is what I call the psychic sucker punch. This is a condition that occurs when someone very sensitive to psychic energy is caught off guard by an intense burst of it. It happens when the psychic is not expecting anything supernatural to occur. They are then blindsided by an intense energetic experience that can throw them off balance. I experienced it during my first investigation of the Upstairs Lounge, as detailed in my book, *Tales From The French Quarter*.

I unwittingly walked into a very strong residual haunting from a tragic fire twenty years earlier. My intent was to only capture some video footage but instead I began to channel and see visions from the tragedy. I became physically ill from the smell of smoke as if I had really inhaled it. Prior to this experience, I didn't know the repercussions of exposing myself to severely traumatized locations.

My friend and fellow psychic, Phillip Humphries, visited Alcatraz Prison on a recent trip to San Francisco. Having made numerous trips to the area, he was well aware of the intense spirit activity there, especially in and around the bay. It has been said that the Golden Gate Bridge connects the worlds of the living and the dead. Since the bridge opened in 1937, it has had more than 1,000 suicides descend from the 4,200-foot suspensions into the bay. During its construction, ten construction workers fell from scaffolds busting through safety nets and plunging into the frigid water. Later in the 1800s, the clipper ship *Tennessee* and her crew disappeared into a dense fog never to be seen again. A phantom ship has been seen passing below the bridge, unmanned.

The maximum-security facility situated on an island in the middle of the bay, which was opened in 1933. The prison was home to some of America's most dangerous criminals. Among its most celebrated was Chicago crime boss, Al Capone, who inhabited numerous prisons in various parts of the country at one time or another. Inmates spent only one hour a day outside their cells. Violating prison rules could mean months of solitary confinement in "The Hole", a tiny cell with no light.

Phillip always reported feeling uneasy around the bridge and bay but on the day he visited Alcatraz, distracted by accompanying friends, his guard was down. At first, it was merely another tourist attraction to him. Suddenly, he became overwhelmed with fear and anxiety. He felt dizzy and disoriented. He heard voices and saw flashes of prisoners in cellblocks.

The onslaught of extreme psychic energy overpowered him. He completely forgot that he was with other people at the location. He ran out of the facility and became so disoriented he barely remembered where he was. He hopped into a cab and composed himself once he left the area. Simultaneously to his initial sucker punch, I was getting out of my van at my daughter's house and suddenly got feelings of panic, "Phillip!" I thought. I knew something was going on with him. Days later, he recounted the event to me.

It's important for everyone going into an actively haunted location to at all times be grounded and protected from unexpected jolts of intense psychic activity. It is equally important that all involved properly ground and cleanse themselves after exposure to such situations.

It is obvious the importance of having psychics on an investigation. In fact, equipment failure is common in the most active areas during an investigation. Cameras sometimes stop completely; batteries in other devices become instantly drained. Sometimes, the psychic connection is the only hope of getting any kind of documentation on a haunted location. There have been numerous times when this has happened. In one building in North Carolina where a little girl and her father were killed in a fire, we felt a strange energy in the hallway that made both of us involved in the investigation feel as if we were turned sideways. Yet, no phenomena appeared on meters or in photographs. No one can explain why sometimes equipment show no sign of phenomena yet psychic experiences occur. But it does serve to prove the importance of the psychic in paranormal investigations.

Communication With The Other Side

Mediums often use direct communication through channeling. The spirit uses the body and sometimes even the voice of the medium to communicate. In today's séances, great care is taken by the medium to not only insure that he or she will be open to channel the spirit but to also protect herself/himself from negative energy that could be picked up. A rigorous preparation is involved when planning to channel. Special herbs are used in baths to open up for channeling. Prior to the baths, the medium must take several days to cleanse the aura. Alternating baths of sea salt and baking soda help in this process. Sandalwood oil can be worn to clear negative energy. Sage smudge and sweet grass are burned to remove negative energy as well. It is also a good idea to do an internal cleanse using juices, teas and fresh fruit several days prior to the séance.

Candles are anointed with oils to enhance the connection. Wormwood oil is great for this purpose, but it is important to note that gloves must be worn to protect the skin from the toxic oil. Wormwood and other herbs are burned with charcoal to draw the spirits.

It is not necessary to have a certain number of people or to hold hands during a séance. It was once believed that it was important to "keep the connection" by holding hands. However, I have channeled spirits on my own with no one there to create a circle. This can be helpful when trying to manifest a spirit outside of a medium, but for channeling, again, not necessary.

The main purpose of the circle when involving several people is to help to focus the energy of all participating. It only takes one person in a room that is not focused or has scattered energy to completely botch a spirit's attempt to come through. The last thing you want is competitive energy going on that will block the spirit. By the same token, it only takes one person who is an open channel to draw in the spirit. If you get a situation where there are several mediums present, the likeliness of bringing the spirits in are greater.

When channeling spirits, the medium not only allows the spirit to speak through them but sometimes the medium will speak in a different voice than their own or even take on the physical characteristics of the person they are channeling.

One thing that all mediums have in common is that channeling can be extremely tiring. If you find that you do have the gift for channeling, it is vital to get adequate rest after a session. Many psychics will become ill after channeling. This is usually not a major health challenge if you properly take care of yourself. I do not channel on a regular basis. I would consider this a compromise to my health so I only do it when necessary. I try to keep myself shielded from accidental channeling situations.

After a channeling session, or for that matter, after any psychic session, I usually ground myself by eating something substantial like steak. I also make sure that for the next couple of days I get extra sleep. In addition, I do a good cleansing using sage and salt to get rid of any residual energy that I might have picked up during the session. I also make sure I burn black candles anointed in sandalwood oil to disburse any negative energy simultaneously with white candles to draw in new positive energy. This along with a good diet and adequate rest will ensure that there are no ill effects from taking in the spirit through channeling.

The important thing to keep in mind when communicating with spirits is to be receptive to what they are saying. If you are too consumed with trying to analyze every little thing or rationalize phenomena you will only block what you are attempting to accomplish. It is always recommended to have another person to help confirm what you are receiving until one is adept in communication methods.

Another wise thing to do is to use different tools to enable communication. I use a variety of tools to cross-reference and confirm my findings that helps reduce the margin for error. This is especially true when communicating with someone who was close, because sometimes the desire to "hear what we want to hear" will create false findings. The subconscious mind is extremely powerful and sometimes your own will can create false paranormal findings only because you want them so strongly. This is why when I do investigations; I generally stick to using a team of people trained in various areas and psychics who work on different levels.

There is a lot of controversy over the use of communication boards, commonly referred to as Ouija boards. I call them communication boards because many different manufacturers make them under many different trade names. The name Ouija board was used by Parker Brothers and sold as a kid's game, ironically. I have been working with boards for many years. I have never had a negative situation arise from working with them. The movie "The Exorcist" revolved around a demon possession that began with a young girl using a communication board. There seems to be a misconception by many that these tools will cause a person to be "possessed". I have never seen anyone become possessed by a demon or any other spirit by using a communication board. The exception would be, those intentionally opening themselves up to spirits or using the communication board while intoxicated or under the influence of drugs. Certain magic rituals that call up spirits invoking them to possess would also pose a danger. Usually, simply using the board as a tool to ask benign questions is perfectly safe.

Communication boards can be very valuable tools when attempting to communicate with the spirit world. When I use them, I also incorporate the use of a digital audio recorder. I have found in most cases, the answers I am getting on the board are reinforced by EVP that is being picked up by the recorder.

While doing the investigation at the Myrtles Plantation, we communicated using both tools with several spirits during the evening. We picked up EVP during these sessions that correlated directly with the answers that we received on the boards.

Another way I have used the boards is in conjunction with someone else doing automatic writing. In my first book, I told of a story that took place in St. John Parish near my home.

In 1915, Julia Brown, who was suspected of being a Voodoo practitioner, made a very bizarre prediction. She was known to sit on her front porch and sing a song about when she died she would take the entire town of what was then Frenier with her. She died in September of 1915. On the day of her funeral the hurricane of 1915 hit Lake Pontchartrain forcing a thirty-foot tidal surge and one hundred mile an hour winds across the tiny town and three other surrounding farm towns. There were only a handful of survivors. Many of whom passed on within a few short years. The victims of the storm were buried along with Julia in a mass grave in what is now the Manchac Swamp. One of the survivors was a young girl who grew up and had a family in the nearby town of Laplace.

The land she and her family once owned is now a subdivision. The developer called me to investigate phenomena that were happening in their newly built home. One of the most frightening happenings that he and his wife had reported to me was what seemed like hurricane force winds that would blow through the home and the sounds of a woman laughing in the master bedroom.

During the investigation, I set up a communication board in one room and another investigator, Kriss Stephens Taylor, doing automatic writing in another. Her communications matched up completely with mine. Through this cross-referencing, we were able to determine that the Schlosser family had once owned the property. Mrs. Schlosser was the little girl who survived the hurricane of 1915! Her son had committed suicide on the property and many of his belongings including a family Bible were left there. I informed the property owners that the best thing to do would be to remove the personal belongings. Once they had done this, the haunting ceased to bother them.

There are many instances when spirits communicate with us without us even trying; sometimes to send a message, perhaps dealing with unfinished business between us. There are countless times that spirits appear and communicate in some way or another in the first few hours of crossing over. This could be a way for some to say goodbye and let loved ones know that they are still ok.

Many religions include communication with spirits as a daily part of their belief system. In the Voodoo tradition, close ties with the ancestors remain in this world as well as the spirit world. Altars are made to the ancestors in homes and family members place food and other favorites of that person on the altar. Common items that might go on an ancestor's altar would be their favorite cologne, favorite piece of jewelry, or favorite flower. Most altars include favorite foods and drink. It is believed that the spirits continue to enjoy the same things in the afterlife as they did during their mortal life. For instance, if someone loved chocolate cake during their life, they would continue to love it in the afterlife. Chocolate cake would be put on that person's altar. As long as the food on the altar continues to look fresh, the spirit is still enjoying it. When the food spoils, it is presumed that the spirit is ready for a replacement. I have seen food last on Voodoo altars for weeks or sometimes months that would have molded on my counter within a few days.

It is believed in many traditions besides Voodoo that the ancestors remain connected with us throughout our lives. They become after death what some might call guardian angels, for lack of a better comparison. The ancestors guide and protect us in our daily lives. In these traditions, communication with the dead is as routine as having a conversation with a living person. Rather than a belief that the spirits go far away to some other mystical place, it is believed that the spirit world is parallel to ours.

These spirits ebb and flow through our world while touching our lives and watching over us.

Fine Tuning Your Psychic Abilities

Many people write to me asking how they might increase their awareness to psychic phenomena. The first step is the desire to do so. In simply expressing interest, the process of opening up that part of the brain and becoming more receptive to psychic phenomena begins. I often tell people "be careful what you wish for". I say this because the subconscious mind is extremely sensitive to the power of suggestion. We all get want we want, most of the time. We may not realize it when it is something our conscious mind isn't aware that we wanted it. To many people this concept would fall into the category of magic.

Magic is nothing more than thoughts, desires, or beliefs manifesting on the physical plane. What we believe IS. If you focus your mental energy on something long enough, it will come into manifestation at some point. That is why it is important to be specific. If you truly desire to become more psychic, you will but you have to believe it. Just as the subconscious mind can manifest that which we want, it can also sabotage the same with negative thought forms, such as "I can't". Desiring to become psychic plus believing that you can paves the way for that door to open for you.

Exercise One: Meditation

Meditation plays an important part of developing psychic abilities. For the beginner, mental focusing is extremely important. If the mind is full of thoughts of daily activities, stresses, and random inner dialogue, this will hinder tapping into your psychic resources. This especially holds true for people who tend to be more analytical. The left-brain can easily talk the self out of anything that cannot be explained through rational means.

The second step in creating an open mind to psychic phenomena is to stop thinking. When I studied Gestalt therapy many years ago, I was often told "lose your mind and come to your senses". Analytical people have a tendency to stay in their minds a lot and be somewhat disconnected from the rest of their senses as well as their physical bodies. Many people are stuck in their heads without even realizing it. We live in a highly stressful environment where we are required to think, evaluate, and analyze everything we encounter. In order to connect to the subtler right brain, we must let go of the internal chatter and find a quieter place inside.

Meditation is a state in which we quiet the mind. There are countless exercises that can help one attain this state of mental calm. It is important to find a place in your home where you cannot be disturbed. Obviously you must also choose a time where you can separate yourself from the rest of your life.

I find that very late at night works best for me. You don't want to be interrupted by ringing phones, doorbells, pets, family members needing attention, or any other distraction that might take you away from being in the moment. It can be indoors or outdoors; some people even find it very relaxing to soak in the bath while meditating.

I incorporate other rituals into my meditations, because that is what works best for me. I always recommend doing an intense cleansing before beginning meditations. Cosmic "junk" attaches itself to our auras and can interfere with our abilities to be clear. We all pick up energetic debris throughout our daily lives. If you are working with spirits or planning to do so, it is particularly important to cleanse yourself regularly to prevent energy from others clinging to you.

Cleansings are relatively easy and inexpensive. You can purchase sea salt at any health food store to use in a bath. Salt neutralizes negativity and removes any energetic residuals picked up from other people and situations. I put a handful of sea salt into a warm bath and soak in it. Submerge your entire body including your head and hair in the salt water. If you have never done a cleansing before, I would suggest doing it for at least a week or two to rid yourself of years of "collecting".

I also burn black and white candles during the bath. Many people are under the misconception that black candles are used in magical practices to do harmful spells. This couldn't be further from the truth.

Color therapy has been proven to be beneficial for the body, mind and spirit. The color black reverses negativity and disburses it back from whence it came. It clears the way for fresh energy to come through. The white candle is for drawing fresh, healing energy that replaces that which has been disbursed. As you soak in the salt water, visualize dirty, negative energy leaving your bodies and white light energy replacing it. Visualize the white light enveloping your entire being, surrounding you and sealing you off from negative energy.

After the bath, use sage smudge to further clear off residual negative energy that might be around you. I prefer white sage followed up with sweet grass. White sage is rare and difficult to find sometimes as it is endangered so again, it depends on what is available to you and what your preferences are. I then follow it with sandalwood oil. Sandalwood oil is good for ridding negative energy. I also use sandalwood oil before working with spirits just to protect myself. I always follow up any spirit encounter, whether it is investigation or communication, with a total cleansing.

Once you have established the best place and time to remove yourself from everything else, sit or lie down quietly and think of nothing. Thinking of nothing is a lot easier said than done. Thoughts constantly race through our minds every second of the day. You must train the mind to shut off thoughts through meditation.

The best way to accomplish this is to direct your mind to the now; what is happening in the present moment. Close your eyes and concentrate on your breathing. Deep breathing techniques create not only relaxation but also bring more oxygen to the organs and help rid the body of toxins. Many people do not think of the lungs as an organ of elimination but that is exactly what they are. Just as you visualized toxic energy leaving and being replaced with white light, the lungs rid the body of toxins through exhalation while replacing fresh oxygen into the bloodstream.

Proper breathing techniques are important to obtain the full benefits of deep breathing. Very few people realize what proper breathing techniques are. Many people are not only breathing in reverse but are using only a portion of their lungs' capacities. Most people think that when they inhale, their stomachs are pulled in and the stomach releases during exhalation; when in fact this is the opposite. One of the best examples of proper breathing is to watch a baby breathe.

As you breathe in, take in as much air as you can, filling the lungs completely. Feel your ribs expand and do not try to hold in your belly. The abdomen area will naturally expand, as does the rib cage. Inhale through the nose. As soon as the lungs are full, and I usually count to four while inhaling, immediately exhale slowly to the count of four. As you exhale, pull the abdomen in which pushes the diaphragm up forcing the air out of the lungs. Empty the lungs completely.

Never breathe rapidly as this can cause hyperventilation. Breathe slowly and steadily. As you do, concentrate on the breath. Think of nothing else. Experience the entire breath and become aware of the feeling as your rib cage stretches as the lungs fills. If you are focused on what your body is doing and focusing on the breath, your mind will automatically become quiet. The best way that I have found to train one's self on quieting the mind for meditation is to focus only on the breathing.

Quieting the mind brings your entire being into the now. There are no thoughts on the day's events or what needs to be done, or what you may have forgotten to do. Stress leaves the body and is replaced by relaxation. It is best to do this exercise with the eyes closed so as not to become distracted. Not only does this assist with improving your psychic abilities but also it is a great way to help overall health. Stress is a leading cause of disease and death; meditation is way of ridding the body from stress.

Once you are able to find that place where the mind is quiet, you will be making contact with your senses. You will become aware of subtle body sensations that you normally would not have noticed. You will feel tension and tightness leaving the muscles. You should meditate at least fifteen minutes a day.

Once you have achieved this quieting of the mind, add what is called a white light meditation. In a seated position, hold your left palm facing upwards to draw in universal energy. Your right palm is faced downwards to expel the old energy back into the ground. As you breathe, visualize a beam of white light coming down from the sky and through your hand. Imagine this warm, white light going through every cell of your body. As you do this, imagine also that a blue light (you can visualize any color you prefer) is leaving your other hand and being sent into the ground. Much as the air enters the lungs as oxygen and leaves as carbon dioxide, so does the energy. Visualize your entire body being surrounded by this white light. So now you are concentrating on the breath and the light. This should be practiced every day for at least fifteen minutes.

Be aware that when you do this sort of meditation you are actually shifting the energy in your body. These meditations should not be done directly after a meal as the energetic shift can cause nausea.

Exercise Two: Feeling Energy

Another exercise is to learn what energy feels like. Sit comfortably and hold the hands facing each other about an inch and a half apart. You should feel a tingling sensation at first; this is the subtle energy of the hands hitting against one another. After a few seconds, you should be able to pulse the hands slightly together and feel the energy between. This usually has somewhat of a spongy feel to it. As you continue to pulse the hands, each time separate them slightly more apart. The energy between will begin to grow. You will feel tingling in the fingers and a slight sensation of "needles and pins" as the energy shoots from the fingers and hands. After a few sessions of this exercise, you should be able to move the hands to about five or six inches apart and still feel the energy from one another. If you cup the hands, you can form it into a ball.

Another exercise to train yourself to feel energy is to feel the energy in trees. I used oak trees because they were large and the energy was more easily picked up. Hold your hands about three inches away from the tree. Within a few seconds, you will feel the energy generating from the tree just as the energy from your hands held together. Feel the energy of the trees coming into your body, refreshing and renewing you.

By doing these exercises on a regular basis, you are training your hands to pick up subtle energetics. You can even train your eyes to see it. Look at any living thing; it can be a plant or animal. The larger the being, the easier it will be to see the energetic body around it. Stare at it for a few moments and then gradually soften your focus. Let the object that you are focusing on slowly go out of focus. Notice the thin, almost transparent outline illuminating from it. This is what is being felt. It is the energetic body.

Continued practice with this exercise can gradually bring about seeing the aura in which colors outlining the energetic body can be seen as well. This, of course, takes much more time to perfect.

Exercise Three: Guessing Games

I call this exercise guessing games because one of the more popular ways people go about training themselves to be more psychic is through card guessing. Some people use regular playing cards. There are numerous tools that can be bought that are the same thing. These consist of a group of cards with symbols on them and you try to match the cards. The cards are faced down and you pick each one up trying each time to select two matching cards. This is much like the match games you can buy for small children. Other guessing games are done with two people; one picks a card and the other tunes in psychically and attempts to guess what card the person is holding.

In many cases, such as my own, psychic abilities are not something one can turn off and on. More often than not, particularly for someone who is either very busy or is new to working with psychic energy, it is more spontaneous. I find that my psychic abilities are much more intense when I am not thinking about it. The less attention I pay with my mind, the more I am in tune. This seems to be true with many people. Thus card-guessing games do not work. The analytical mind takes over and the individual winds up using that side of the brain rather than the psychic side.

Exercise Four: Candles

One of the best ways to help develop your psychic skills is to build on the ability to not only keep all thought from drifting through the mind but to also be able to focus on one thing.

Once you have mastered focusing on your breathing through meditation, try meditating with a candle. Instead of focusing on the breath and the body, you focus on the flame of the candle. Stare intently at the flame, eventually softening your focus. Eventually, through concentration you should be able to make the flame rise and fall with the use of your mind.

For some, this could even be a prerequisite to using your mind to move objects. Do not expect to do this overnight, however. This sort of movement of psychic energy takes a great deal of time to perfect. But if time is something you have a lot of as well as the desire to perform such feats, then you can achieve this level of psychic control.

One important thing to always remember is to trust your intuition. Most of the time when you get a feeling about something; you are right. Many people contact me regarding questions about loved ones who have passed on. I often hear people describe situations where they believe a love one has tried to contact them. I usually tell them if it feels that the love one was visiting them, they probably were.

It is human nature to attempt to convince the self that it was a coincidence or a figment of the imagination. If you sense a presence of a spirit, more than likely you are really experiencing it. Furthermore, if you are sensing a presence and feel that it is someone that you knew, more than likely it is that spirit trying to make communication with you.

From there, you might want to go on and attempt using a communication board or even trying your hand at automatic writing. If you do decide to do this, here are a few helpful hints.

Hints:

1. When placing your hand on the pen or disk of the board, always use a very light touch. Allow the spirit to control the tool rather than your own will.

2. I recommend using your hand that is controlled by the psychic side of your brain. Usually this would be the left hand. Sometimes for left-handed people, this might be the right hand.

3. Trust your intuition. Whatever the first thing you feel comes to mind, go with it.

4. Talk to the spirit as if it is a real person.

5. Stick to asking questions that require a "yes" or "no" answer. This is very important. It is difficult for spirits to break through and communicate on our plane. Don't expect sophisticated answers. If not a yes/no question, keep it limited to answers that only require one word.

6. Always ask a question that would identify the spirit. Ask a question that only that person would be able to answer. This eliminates the possibility of communicating with someone else and being fooled. Some spirits enjoy "playing" with those of us here; don't assume they are all honest. Just as there are pranksters and cons in this life, the same holds true for spirits. Whatever personality a person had during their life will continue within the spirit realm.

7. Always treat the spirit with respect. Do not resort to yelling or cursing at the spirit. This will result in it not cooperating with you. Also, respect when the spirit grows tired of communicating and wishes to stop.

8. Never allow a spirit that is communicating with you to do divination. Many a foolish person has used a communication board to tell the future. Spirits do not necessarily know what is going to happen to you, although some may. It is best to keep communication about information rather than to rely on advice from a spirit that you do not know. The only exception would be in the case where you are positive that the spirit you are speaking to be an ancestor and is warning you of something for your protection. Always be certain before taking advice from a spirit. In the instance where it may be a warning, it is best to seek professional help from a qualified psychic to confirm such advice.

9. Never use communication tools to evoke or invoke spirits who were never human. Dabbling with elementals or demons can be dangerous business. Don't allow fear or negative thoughts to stop you from reaching your full psychic potential. Always remember whatever you seek usually finds you.

What Do They Want?

Some ghosts appear to certain people for specific reasons. I have experienced countless cases wherein the visitations seem to have a purpose and the trick is figuring out what it is.

When I worked on the local television show, "Haunted New Orleans," one episode focused around an elderly woman who was, in her opinion, being terrorized by the ghost of a little girl. The woman reported waking in the middle of the night and seeinga small girl standing by her bed. The child had something in her hand and was trying to hand it to the woman.

I sent a team of paranormal investigators who caught a large orb on video. The bouncing ball of light was recorded as it glided up the stairs then down the hallway and into the bedroom. It hovered over the bed momentarily then darted out of the room. The investigation concluded that an entity was visiting the woman but still did not explain why.

Only through questioning the client was I able to piece together what was happening. The woman had been a pediatric nurse for over fifty years. The child ghost was probably a patient of hers and trying to give her something. I encouraged her to take whatever it was in the girl's hand the next time she appeared but the woman was still too afraid.

I also believe that because of her age and state of health that she was nearing death herself and the veil was becoming thinner for her. When we are closer to the other side, we have more exposure to it and consequently see more than we once did.

At the H. H. Whitney Bed & Breakfast several ghosts remained in the property, all of who were the original owners. Three siblings, two brothers and an older sister owned the house.

The three lived in the house their entire lives. The eldest cared for her brothers until they passed away, then she herself eventually died on the property as well. Every psychic that had visited the home came up with the name "Emily."

As it turned out, the current owner found records and photographs in the attic and the one of the original owners' names was Amelia, which is German for Emily.

The current owners were a male couple and it is believed that Amelia relates to them as she did her two brothers. She continues to watch over them.

During the investigation the EMF meter started going off in certain areas of the house. This would not have been unusual except my meter has a button that has to be held down in order to turn it on. The meter was going off in Glenn's hand, one of the owners, while it was not being physically enabled. We also burned through numerous batteries that kept draining throughout the investigation but only when Glenn handled the equipment.

During filming of this investigation, I had my daughter, Stephanie, with me. As we filmed in one room, I happened to notice out of the corner of my eye that she was standing in the hallway with her eyes wide and her hands over her mouth. She was pointing at something down the hallway. When I asked her about it she described a man wearing a dark suit with dark hair who appeared to be angry. Later that night, two of my paranormal investigators, Jonathan and Adam, found one of the photo albums of the original owners. One photo was that of a man who fit that description. When we showed the photograph to Stephanie, she exclaimed, "That's him! He's the angry man."

We believe these spirits remain to look over the property and are quite content doing so. The man might have been angry at all the equipment and activity cluttering up the home, as he didn't seem to be a malevolent haunting.

Not all ghosts who are earthbound are stuck here. Some stay for unfinished business then move on when they are ready. Such is the case with Cadillac's Bar and Grill in Laplace, Louisiana. The owner, Vincent, had been a friend of mine for many years. He contacted me in November 2011, and told me that he had a ghost that was literally chasing off his employees. Vincent was a very rational person and certainly not an alarmist. If he was that upset over the activity, I had to believe it was serious.

Vincent believed he had several entities haunting his club. One former owner had died from a stroke four months earlier. This man had a loft above the men's bathroom that he used to take naps if he was working a long shift at the club. Recently, employees reported seeing the men's room door open and shut on its own at various times. Some reported seeing the figure of a man walking in and out who would vanish as soon as anyone noticed him. Since this person had died very recently, it was reasonable to assume that he would probably hang around for a short while, and then move on.

Although many hauntings wind up being former owners who prefer to stay attached to a property that feels familiar, as in the case of the H. H. Whitney House, others become attached to a property for completely different reasons. When spirits continue to dwell in what they consider to be their home, they cannot be removed until, of course, they are ready.

The other ghost was also male, but much younger. He kept appearing in the office and in the ice room of the club. It was a bit harder to figure out who he might be. Vincent knew that there had been some shootings in the club back in the 1980s. There had also been a fire, which burned down the original building.

I pulled the history of the property and found that the property was once the location of the roadside attraction, the Snake Farm. My older brother used to take me to the Snake Farm when I was a small child. This place had every type of reptile imaginable. Inside the main building was a massive pit where huge anacondas and pythons were on display.

The Snake Farm closed down in the early 1980s shortly after the owner's niece was bitten by a king cobra and died. The old building was torn down and a nightclub was built in its place; then replaced after it burned down. I sifted through articles trying to find a death at the location that might fit the description of the younger man's ghost.

As I continued my research, the ghostly activity increased in the club. Late at night after closing, employees witnessed the large fans turn on without assistance. One bartender, Leah, was grabbed on the shoulders but when she turned no one was there. The ghost seemed to be attracted to one employee in particular, a young man named Hunter. A vast majority of the activity usually occurred on Hunter's shifts.

One evening as Hunter stocked up one of the refrigerators in the ice room, he looked up and saw reflected in the mirrored doors, a young man with long hair standing over him. He quickly turned, but no one was there. Hunter gave a detailed description to Vincent. Vincent had done some of his own research and finally realized who the ghost had been.

On December 17, 2011, a band called Misbehavin' was scheduled to play their thirty year anniversary show. It was to be their last show together. Twenty years ago, on the day before Thanksgiving, the band had played at the club. The keyboard player had taken off early that evening.

The following day was to be his wedding day. While on break, he told everyone good night. He gathered his equipment and departed through the side stage door. Unbeknownst to him, a drunken patron had also left the club, out through the front doors. The woman got into her car and pulled out onto Airline Highway, going in the wrong direction. When she realized she was heading into ongoing traffic, she swerved into the side parking lot; just as the keyboard player was exiting. He never saw her coming. He was killed upon impact. Vincent was convinced that this keyboard player was his ghost.

When Vincent discussed his theory with me, I agreed. The recent activity began right around the anniversary of the man's death and the upcoming show had something to do with it. Time was of the essence. I felt certain that once the show took place, the man would move on. If any documentation were to be done, it had to happen before the show. I contacted Terri Kilpatrick who worked with the ghost hunting organization, Louisiana Spirits to conduct an investigation. Terri rallied her troops together and planned an overnight investigation the Friday before the show. Hunter arranged to stay with the group that evening.

Terri emailed me her findings, "We were there from 2:00 AM till 7:15 AM. I did get a couple of pictures with a smoky haze. Which was only weird because when that happened I started coughing, then two others coughed too. I'd quit smoking five years ago and I have a hard time being around people who smoke now. We asked the question, 'do you smoke?' on the recorder just in case.

I saw a shadow man to the right of the stage three times. He walked from right to left from the door. It happened after I had taken a few pictures, but nothing appeared on the photos. We heard the sound of a piano as if someone hit two keys coming from the stage. This was also caught on tape. I felt something brush up behind me in the cooler room twice. I was the only one in there. While in the cooler room I heard very soft music coming from right outside the door. I heard it again later that night after going in that room again. I found out afterward that the cleaning lady had the same experience. One of the girls on my team kept getting into cold spots around her and felt her hair pulled.

I had Hunter sit in the back corner and ask some questions. I had him hold different meters and recorders. During his conversation, the temperature gage went up and down and the K2 Meter went off. Hunter asked the ghost what kind of liquor he liked, naming off several brands. When he asked, 'Do you like Captain Morgan?' The K2 lit up all three lights."

Another member of her group wrote in, "I experienced chills and cold sensations near my spine. I was constantly questioning my hearing ability because I heard a piano play on to different occasions. I also felt like at one point when we were asking questions that someone was trying to stroke my head or hair."

On the night of the show, I took photographs throughout the club. I took several repetitive shots around the keyboard. In one of the middle shots, I picked up some ectoplasm whisking around the keyboard player. I later interviewed one of the band members who was close the deceased man. He told me that he was to be the best man in his wedding. He also admitted that on the night he was killed, when he said good night and hugged him, he had a look on his face as if he would never see him again. After the show I stayed on a bit at the club, telling the spirit that it was ok for him to move on now.

Several weeks later, I checked with Hunter who reported that the activity had quieted down. I have no doubt that the ghost was indeed that of the keyboard player and he wanted to be a part of that last show. To my knowledge, he has not returned to the club.

It seems that many people on some unconscious level know when they are getting ready to leave. In older persons who are sickly and near death's door, they begin to have visions of other loved ones who have passed before them.

In 1998, my first book about ghosts came to completion. As I sat at a book signing waiting for customers, a woman with a familiar face entered the door. As she walked past me she looked at my face and stopped. She stared at me a while as if she knew me but wasn't sure. She said, "From where do I know you?" I recognized the face but couldn't quite place her. Then I suddenly remembered. She was a former teacher who had instructed me in

Subtle Body Energetics. She looked tired and sad. Her eyes were dull and filled with a hopeless look. I barely recognized her.

She asked what I was doing in the store. I showed her my book and explained that I was no longer working in my bodywork practice. I went on to explain that I had begun to use my knowledge of energy to work with those who had passed on to the spirit world. Suddenly, her eyes lit up and a smile slightly graced her face. It was if a burden had been taken of her. She explained that she felt it was meant for her to run in to me there on that day. Her daughter had recently died and she had been struggling to accept her passing on. She was desperately seeking a source to help her in communicating with her daughter. She believed that I could help her. I agreed that it was more than coincidence that we crossed paths.

She went into detail how her daughter, several years before had described seeing a portal in the sky on one full moon night. The child had exclaimed, “Look! That is the way out of here!” I explained to her ways to communicate with her child. The conversation I had with her, however brief, seemed somehow to give her comfort. I gave her my contact information but never heard from her again.

The Crisis Apparition

A crisis apparition is an apparition that appears shortly before or after death or at the precise time of death. I have found that these recently departed spirits can appear to take care of any unfinished business and say goodbye for several days after death.

These types of hauntings do not mean that the person's spirit is "trapped" on the earth plane or that they are going to remain earthbound for an extended period of time. These spirits remain earthbound long enough to visit loved ones, say their goodbyes, and give last minute messages to those who were emotionally close to them, then they move on. Many believe that all spirits stop in and say goodbye or give messages but that's not necessarily the case. This belief often leads to disappointment when a loved one passes. Of the ones who do, this manifestation can appear in various forms.

A common theme for the crisis apparition is to awaken to find a departed loved one sitting on the edge of the bed wanting to speak. Other themes include symbols manifesting that have particular meaning to the departed and the receiver and there can also be dream manifestations.

In the movie, “Dragonfly”, the departed wife communicates with her husband through symbols, usually dragonflies. This symbol had meaning to the woman during her life and her husband was aware of it. After my brother passed away, many people began to see hummingbirds. But the hummingbirds appeared only to those who were aware that it was his favorite bird. I, on the other hand, saw tree frogs that had their own special meaning to me.

Spirits communicating through dreams is very common. I have learned to distinguish when my dreams are merely my dreams and when there are spiritual messages being transmitted. The more in tune one is to receiving messages from spirit, the better one can interpret the nature of these dreams; as with the case, when my friend Gary passed away.

Several months before his untimely death, he visited me in a dream. He was seated on the edge of my bed and told me that he would be leaving soon and he was not coming back. He relayed to me that he didn’t want to go without saying something to me.

When I awoke, I was not sure how to interpret what I had experienced. He had on many occasions mentioned possibly moving away and of course my immediate thought was that he might be moving soon. I didn’t want to believe that the dream was a premonition of his passing away. The dream was so real, so vivid. I knew that he really did appear to convey the message for a reason so I shared it with a fellow psychic. She warned me to prepare myself for the worst. Never did I mention the dream to my friend. I simply put it aside and prayed that he would only move away rather than leave this world.

Several months later I was awakened about 4 AM on a Saturday morning by some spirit urging me to finish this book without changing it. This spirit was adamant. I couldn't see or audibly hear its voice but it kept sending messages into my mind, "Keep the book the way it is, just add to it."

Needless to say, I could not get back to sleep. I immediately pulled up the old book and began to go through the chapters.

"Whoever you are, you're right," I told the spirit.

I spent the next several days working on my original version of the book. Having ripped it apart for various other projects, it was a tedious process. I dedicated the weekend to the book.

The following Tuesday, I was awakened by a phone call informing me that Gary never woke up the Friday before. It was then that I realized that my dream had been an advance warning of his departure. Although I was deeply saddened by his loss, the shock was lessened by the dream. I also realized at that point that it was his ghost that had me up all weekend writing. He loved the original version of the book; it was one his favorites. We had spent countless hours discussing it and our thoughts on the afterlife.

As the day progressed, I found myself feeling more and more grief-stricken. That evening, I spoke out to his spirit. I told him that although I was grateful that he had already said goodbye to me, I wanted more.

"If anybody can break through and give me a sign, it would be you," I told him.

"I need to know that you are ok with this transition," I called out to him. "I can't come to closure until I know that you are really alright," I ended.

That night, he appeared again in a dream. He didn't look like he did in the last dream like he did in life. His face was very transparent yet he was smiling. His body appeared as bright, colorful streams of energy swirling around me. Behind him was a bright white light. I heard his voice, the voice that was so familiar to me.

"Don't be sad, I don't want anyone to be sad," he said.

He went on, "I am ok. Things happen exactly the way they are supposed to."

"But what happened to you?" I asked tearfully

"It was just my time, that's all," he answered.

His energy swirled around me, blanketing me. I felt nothing but peace and pure love; nothing I've ever experienced in this earthly body; Divine love. I woke up feeling at peace and comforted. There are a lot of skeptics who would rationalize the experience as seeing in a dream what I wanted to see. However, the feeling that I experienced was something that I could barely describe because it was not of this world. And I know it was him without a doubt. I heard his voice, I felt his presence. Nothing can convince me of anything less. I know he found peace.

Others are not so fortunate. When a person dies under stressful conditions, violent or tragic death, untimely death, the transition can be traumatic. Because of this, some spirits remain in the transitional stage longer than they should. Some remain earthbound, clinging to the physical, simply because they were not ready to leave.

Many years ago when I was a student, I completed my required community service hours at Project Lazarus House, a hospice facility for AIDS patients. I was thrown into a situation that surrounded me with death. Most of the residents of the facility were people who had been abandoned by their friends and families who feared the disease. Never had I experienced a place shrouded in such sadness and despair. It was heartbreaking.

For four months, I volunteered to do whatever I could to make these unfortunate souls as comforted as possible during their final days. As benevolent the cause was to provide a nurturing, caring atmosphere for these victims, it was still a house of death. Most of the patients died peacefully. But one poor young man, whose mother was a religious fanatic, had been convinced that he was condemned to hell. He literally left this world kicking and screaming. He was terrified.

None of these individuals were ready to die. Many of them were in the prime of their lives. They were victims of a mystery disease that had no cure and held no hostages. To add insult to injury, family members, friends, and even partners discarded them in their fear and ignorance. Even for the ones who passed without the hysteria, their deaths were lonely ones. Dark, shadowy figures darted about the dreary corridors of the House.

Many years later, I ran into someone who also worked on the project during that time. He admitted to seeing the shadows as well. These were not malevolent spirits, just ones that still felt the loneliness, isolation, sadness, and anger that their lives were cut short and that their loved ones forgot them even before they left this world.

My Shining Moment

People always ask me, “What is the weirdest thing you’ve ever encountered?”

I have to admit that most recently it was what I have come to refer to as a “Shining” moment. Who could ever forget that memorable scene in “The Shining” when Jack Nicholson’s character meets Lloyd the bartender? Nicholson walks into the empty Gold Room and flips on the lights. As he mentally crumbles, Lloyd appears before a full liquor bar.

It was a typical Tuesday evening as I pulled onto Toulouse Street and made my way to the last block where I knew I could find parking. The one and only parking space was in front of a bar called The Recovery Room. I had been parking on that block for many years and never noticed an operating bar there so it seemed odd. A young man stood out front and two men were seated inside drinking. As I exited my vehicle, the man walked towards me and told me that he would love to have our tour material in his business. I thanked him and told him I’d send someone over with tour brochures.

He then asked me if I wanted to see something weird. "How weird could it be?" I wondered to myself.

I followed him to the back of the bar. He told me that a former owner had an indoor swimming pool installed in the back room. He apparently ran his own private Turkish bathhouse. The young man brought me to a room with artwork covering the walls. He removed one of the paintings revealing a darkened room on the other side. Inside, I saw several Grecian-looking statues and columns. There was a large marble slab on the floor. He told me that under the marble was a pool.

"Wow, that is pretty weird," I told him.

He told me that he believed that the building was haunted. He said that he often spent the nights working on his art in the back room. He gave details of hearing footsteps and his dog barking at something behind the wall. I offered to research the history and conduct an investigation. I then explained that I had to get to work but I would send some brochures over to him. I walked out onto Toulouse Street about twenty paces then turned onto Chartres Street.

Right before me, a co-worker was getting some promotional materials from his trunk. I immediately asked him to bring some brochures to the new bar around the block. He agreed then I walked on over to St. Peter Street where we begin our tours.

Several minutes later, my co-worker returned. I asked him if he brought the brochures to the bar and he replied, “Yes, I did but no one was there. There’s just a locked up building there.”

“That’s impossible.” I responded. “I just left the place; there were customers inside. Did you go right away?”

“Of course, as soon as you asked me,” he said.

The young man outside of the bar had given me his phone number. I immediately called it. A generic voice mail answered. I left a message for him to call me about the brochures.

After numerous text and voice messages, we gave up on contacting the man. For several days, we walked past the building in hopes of seeing it open. This went on for five months. The business has never been open since that day I went into it.

We pulled the historic records on the building and found photographs of the room. It was exactly what I saw when I looked on the other side of the painting. The only exception was that in the photographs, the pool was visible.

As it turned out, a friend of mine was a bartender at The Recovery Room for a short while after Katrina. He said that he only worked there for a limited time then the business closed down. He was unaware of anyone reopening the bar.

The bar has since remained locked and I never heard back from the man I had met outside of it. I don’t know why a bar would have been open only for a few minutes then close down permanently. There is no explanation. Several guides began calling it my “Shining Moment.”

Dark Forces

Demons, Guardians, and Elemental Spirits

There are a wide variety of spirits on the spiritual plane that are not your average ghost. Many a ghost hunter makes the mistake of thinking that all paranormal phenomena are caused by ghosts. Therefore it is important to know the difference.

Some spiritual beings are higher vibrational beings than ghosts. These beings are higher to God's consciousness and were never human. These energies are called many different things throughout different cultures and religions. They usually work on our behalf and aid us in our spiritual enlightenment. They bring us closer to a higher consciousness but not all spirits are ghosts or highly evolved entities. There are darker spirits that are detached from God's conscientiousness - demons.

These darker forces do not necessarily work on our behalf. High ceremonial magicians often call upon these forces for their specific purposes. That call usually requires a price to pay in return for services rendered. Although it is rare, it is quite possible that one can encounter the darker forces while working with ghosts.

Usually if this sort of spirit is present, it will be accompanied with bad odors and a feeling of uneasiness. Several years ago, I did a paranormal investigation of the Buckland Museum of Witchcraft in New Orleans. There was a great deal of negative energy present in the building and the owners were experiencing a variety of disturbances. Unbeknownst to them at the time, one of their employees was doing magical work with demons. The result of this negative work was causing the other employees and owners alike to experience changes in their normal personalities, increased arguments, and sickness. Throughout time, evil spirits have been blamed for pestilence, chaos, and disease.

While conducting the investigation, I became intrigued with one of the exhibits in the museum: a demon trapped in a box. This entity had been captured by Dr. Raymond Buckland many years before and sealed in a wooden box. Prior to its capture, it had plagued a man for years. It destroyed his marriage, his career, and his health before he resorted to an exorcism trapping the demon. In a rather risky experiment, I decided to see if we could obtain a voice from it on a digital recorder.

I shook the box vigorously to entice the demon to respond. I slammed it on the table and yelled at it. Then I left a voice-activated recorder next it and exited the room. When I returned several minutes later and listened to the recording, I was shocked to hear a demonic voice on the recorder shouting out my name.

I do not recommend trying this sort of experiment to anyone who is a novice at working with the occult. I conducted this experiment in a very controlled situation. I was also very careful not to open the wooden box. The demon inside was completely disabled as long as it remained inside. I by no means take demons lightly. If one attaches to a person, it can destroy his or her life. Never invite a demon into your life.

Ancient grimoires or spell books can be purchased in any bookstore. I have heard some practitioners of magic say that these books are harmless and are missing essential "keys" to make the invocations work. This is untrue. There are specific laws in the universe that apply to all regardless of belief systems or religion. One is the *law of attraction.* You will attract to you what you put out. Therefore whatever it is you are seeking, you will draw it to you. Put in simpler terms, if you begin to look for demons, demons will look for you. And they will find you.

Many an innocent person has purchased books on invocation of demons and unwittingly conjured them only to find that they cannot control them. I have encountered numerous people through the years who attempt to "dabble" with the darker forces for amusement only to find something much more diabolical than they ever imagined. Medieval sorcery is not for the untrained magician and especially not for the ghost hunter.

Demon possession can cause people to lose their jobs, it destroys relationships, people can develop addictions to drugs or gambling, and it can cause unexplained illness, which can lead to death. The best rule of thumb where a demon might be involved is, leave it alone. If a person or location is plagued by such an entity it should be left to the qualified priest, priestess or occultist to deal with it.

Not all evil spirits are major demons. There are many otherwise benevolent guardian spirits, such as those who watch over burial grounds, that can be extremely dangerous when riled.

A bizarre case of a ghost not being a ghost is that of the infamous Bell Witch in Adams, Tennessee. In the summer of 2002, I was asked to speak at Katefest, a weekend of investigation of the Bell Witch phenomena. Pat Fitzhugh who hosted the event and had spent years researching the history and the phenomena in Adams contacted me. He arranged for me to not only speak at the event, but to conduct a séance.

I gathered from Pat the history of the haunting. Sometime in the early 1800s John Bell moved his family from North Carolina to Robertson County, Tennessee, settling in a community that later became known as Adams. Bell purchased some land and slaves from an old woman named Kate Batts. After the land was purchased, Kate claimed to have been swindled by Bell and swore her revenge. She died in 1817 and that is when it all began.

Later that year, John Bell was inspecting his fields when he encountered a strange-looking animal sitting in the middle of a cornrow. The animal looked like a dog with the head of a rabbit. He shot at it and it disappeared. Bell thought nothing more about the incident until later that evening, after dinner. He and his family heard "beating" sounds outside of their house. The sounds continued each night, becoming louder. Eventually, the Bell children began to hear what they believed to be rats gnawing at their bedposts. An unseen force pulled at their covers and threw their pillows on the floor as they attempted to sleep each night. The sounds continued and were accompanied by the sounds of an old woman singing hymns and moaning. But it was the Bell's youngest daughter, Betsy, that became the focal point of the evil spirit. She was slapped and her hair pulled, sometimes leaving visible marks on her face and body.

In 1819, General Andrew Jackson, a personal friend of John Bell, paid a visit to the Bell home after hearing of the disturbances. As his men came upon the property, their wagon abruptly stopped. Despite several horses drawing it, nothing could move it. Jackson began to call the spirit a witch. Immediately, a female voice was heard telling them to move on. She also warned that she would see them again later that evening. During the night, one of Jackson's men began screaming; his body thrashed about. From that point on, Jackson called the entity the "Bell Witch". Most of the people in

Adams called her Kate believing it to be the disgruntled spirit of Kate Batts.

Through the years, the Bell family was haunted by the entity. The spirit followed Betsy around, taunting and threatening her. The spirit beat John Bell until he died in 1820. Next to his deathbed was a vial of mysterious liquid. The family gave a bit of it to a cat; it died immediately. John Bell Jr. swore he heard the voice of a woman tell him, "I gave Ol' Jack a big dose of that last night, and that fixed him."

He threw the vial into the fireplace and it exploded into blue flames. As John Bell was buried, the family heard the spirit laughing and singing. After their father's death, the Bell children continued to receive visitations from the spirit throughout their adult lives.

There is much speculation on exactly what the Bell Witch is. During my investigation, I conducted a séance in the area of the former Bell property called the dell. We arrived in the dell via a large wagon pulled by a tractor through a field. We got to the dell and proceeded to make a large circle. I asked all participants to join hands, palm-to-palm. The energy flowed through the circle like a wave of electricity.

Suddenly, we could feel a dark, ominous presence on the outside of the circle. Its breath was heavy as it slowly stood behind each person in the circle. We could all here it's growling. Several people in the circle began to see the image of a large black dog. I knew it was not a dog, but a wolf. I saw an image in my mind's eye of a large wolf with red glowing eyes. It stood on two legs and towered over us. It continued to growl and snarl as it circled us for several minutes.

Eventually, the apparition of a young woman manifested inside the circle. Those who were able saw her wearing a white dress. She was afraid and crying. Within a few short moments, she disappeared. One woman in the group managed to channel her but not long enough to find out whom she might have been.

Shortly thereafter, the wolf-like spirit was also gone. Very little information was obtained from the experience other than we all experienced the dark spirit that circled us. The only thing I was sure of was that this spirit was not a ghost.

We left the dell and began the long ride across the pasture. As the tractor pulled us slowly along, a thick fog rolled up behind us. It seemed to follow our path. In the fog, I could feel the presence of many eyes watching us. It felt as if a pack of wolves were hidden in the fog. One of the participants of the event, a man of Native American descent named James, mentioned he could see red eyes in the fog. I asked him what did he think they were, and he answered, "Wolves."

In speaking with Pat later that evening, I found that through the years the Bell Witch had appeared to a number of people as a large black dog or wolf. I also learned from him that the Bell property had once been land sacred to the Native Americans. Adams, Tennessee was situated right alongside the

Trail of Tears. In researching Native American culture and spiritualism I had learned that there are guardians of the burial grounds. I had interviewed a Native American woman for one of my documentaries that mentioned that these spirits often appear as wolves or jackals.

Another interesting theory is that Native burial grounds contain *portals*. Portals are doorways to the spirit world. Ancient cultures built their burial grounds as well as their sacred ritual spaces on *ley lines;* energy paths that surround the entire earth. The energy that is produced by the intersection of these lines create portals. Ley lines are the earth's power centers. If a person sits or lies over a ley line for an extended time, they will tend to be hyperactive. This can work to an advantage in healing or in situations where extra energy is useful, but if someone is already very energetic, the ley line could cause an unhealthy situation. And if the ley line is negative, the negative aspects of extra energy will be manifested as well. This can cause tension, anxiety, and neurosis in certain people.

Vortices in ley lines are bursts of energy arising from the earth. People who have experienced these bursts of energy will describe feelings of being energized, weaving, floating, or seeing white light. The human body has vortices of its own, the chakras. When the chakras are open and the energy flows freely the body is free of disease and pain. Blocked energy in these vortices is believed to be the cause of imbalance in the body, which eventually causes disease.

Some of the most haunted as well as the spiritual places on earth are at intersections of ley lines. The Pyramids of Giza and Stonehenge for example are strategically placed in such a way. Sedona, Arizona is a perfect example of energy vortices that are produced by ley lines. There are four major features there, including Bell Rock, Cathedral Rock, Boynton Canyon, and Secret Canyon. Bell Rock is believed to be a portal to other dimensions. Anomalous electrical readings have been scientifically documented there.

On the former Bell property there is also a cave that is claimed to be one of the most haunted sites in the country. It is believed that there is a portal near or inside the cave. Inside the cave are sounds that cannot be explained. Cameras break and abnormal forms appear in pictures that are taken. This is all contributed to the burial of Indians in and around the cave.

After the trip to the dell, I was asked to participate in a panel discussion about the Bell Witch. I explained to the group that based on what I had experienced during the séance, I believed that the spirit was not a ghost, nor a witch but a guardian spirit of the sacred grounds. I went on to describe the overwhelming feeling of foreboding that I felt both during the séance and on the trip back from the dell. I concluded that the spirit had been on that land long before the Bells bought the property.

I was convinced that the haunting was due to the disruption brought on by the settling of the white man. It was then that I urged the group not to spend the night in the Bell cabin. It was apparent to me that this spirit did want ghost hunters and curious photographers investigating any further. My warnings were ignored and several ghost hunters spent the night in the cabin the following night. Most of them became violently ill in the middle of night.

Kriss Stephens Taylor conducted the overnight stay. Kriss did an auto-writing session in the Bell Witch cabin. The results showed words scribbled out, "*Leave house*," and "*Go away now.*" It was directly after this session that a man, who had been sound asleep, awoke and vomited profusely on the front porch of the cabin.

There are many instances where people mistake these types of spirits for ordinary ghosts. This is when it is a good idea to know when to back off. Many a determined ghost hunter has become ill or injured in pursuit of ghosts all the while dealing with an entity that is something else. If a spirit is physically attacking someone, causing illness, or otherwise creating extreme negative repercussions in someone's life, leave it alone; you are out of your league. Guardian spirits can be dangerous when provoked. Many an untrained person has tampered with this type of entity, usually by meddling with burial grounds, with very negative results.

If you must research such an area, there are several rules of etiquette one must follow. The first rule is that of reverence. There are many areas in this country where the Native Americans will not go, because of the sacredness to that area. If there is a particular place that you wish to investigate, and you know that Native People stay away from it, know that there is a reason for that and respect it. Find somewhere else to investigate; there are many haunted places to check out. If you do wind up in an area that is sacred, such as a burial ground or cemetery, respect the spirits there. They are referred to as guardians for a reason.

It's always a good idea to ask permission before doing any work in these areas, as well as having the utmost respect for the tombs and headstone.

NEVER TAKE ANYTHING FROM A GRAVE, ESPECIALLY REMAINS!

There are some old cemeteries, especially here in New Orleans, that are run down and from time to time, human bones will surface. Some people think it's cool to run across a bone in a cemetery and like to take back a "souvenir". This is a big mistake.

Several years ago a good friend and co-worker of mine called me in the middle of the night in total fear. After hearing my dissertation on how I hate being awakened in the middle of night, he explained to me that he had found some bones in a cemetery where he had been doing a tour and took them home with him. He also said that a flying black shadowy object hovering over his bed had awakened him. He was terrified. I told him that he needed to return what he had taken. He wrapped up the bones and immediately brought them back to the cemetery as soon as it opened.

Other types of spirits, which have never been human, are *elementals*. Elementals are lower forms of spirit beings that can be quite annoying. There are thousands of nature spirits that exist on the spiritual plane. The go by many names depending on the culture, but some are called nymphs, fairies, gnomes, goblins, or elves.

Elementals are similar to other nature spirits except they are vibrating at a much lower rate, and have no form. A fire elemental may appear as a spark, a face in a candle flame, or a warm spot that you suddenly walk through. A water elemental may be a cold spot. An air elemental could be a sudden breeze or tiny whirlwind in the dust. An unexplained smell or taste could be earth elementals. They are playful and can be disruptive to ordinary life. Elementals cannot be tamed or controlled. They can be dangerous if irritated so it is best to avoid them.

They have no defined personalities but work by symbols and feelings. They are energy with will; they display emotions without being emotional. If a property or person is being plagued with an elemental, as with demons, it is best left to the guidance of an adept occultist or qualified clergy.

Real Vampires

Other types of demon-like spirits are those who feed on the life force of the living, more commonly known as vampires. Most people associate vampires with fictional characters that they have seen in movies or read about in novels; a dramatic caped figure that flies into the bedroom of an unsuspecting victim in the form of a bat. Real vampires are far more complex than the characters associated with them.

Early accounts of vampire attacks in Eastern Europe usually involved a person being visited in their sleep by a deceased family member. More times than not, it appeared in a dream. The victim feels them bearing down on top of them and there is some form of attack.

Very rarely (if ever) is a physical attack involving the drawing of blood mentioned. Clearly it is a spiritual or psychic attack of some kind that is being described. Subsequent attacks usually result in the victim losing vitality, becoming sick, weak, and eventually dying.

Much of the vampire hysteria that spread through Europe from the 1400s until 1900 was based on ignorance of the decomposition process. The victim would describe an attack by the ghost of a deceased family member. The townspeople would exhume the body of that person and make a determination on the condition of the physical body.

During decomposition, the skin shrinks giving the illusion that hair and nails have grown. The body is bloated with gasses making it appear engorged, presumably with blood. When a stake was surged into the heart of the corpse, the mouth would open and the gasses made a noise as if the "creature moaned." Fluids oozed from its orifices as if the blood it had just consumed was flowing out of it. Misunderstanding of these normal phases of decomposition gave rise to legends of a physical creature rising from the grave and drinking the blood of the living.

Certain diseases reinforced this belief. With porphyria, the individual has a shortage of platelets in the blood. Caused by a recessive gene, it was often seen in royalty as they were commonly inbred. The symptoms of this disease include receding gums that make the canines appear elongated. The skin is thin and pale and the patients show signs of photophobia. Eventually, dementia sets in and these patients were known to physically attack others. Drinking blood would lessen the severity of the disease but gave way to it being confused with a physical vampire.

Tuberculosis was another disease blamed on vampirism. One of the most famous American vampire stories is based on a tuberculosis outbreak in Rhode Island in the late 1800s. Mercy Brown was a young girl when various members of her family began to die from what was then called consumption - wasting away.

During these epidemics, entire families would contract the disease. One family member would die. Other members of the family would run high fevers that led to hallucinations. This could explain seeing the recently deceased member visiting in a dream. Victims of tuberculosis feel heaviness in the chest especially upon lying down. This could appear to someone hallucinating with fever that the ghost of another is attacking or smothering the victim. Late stages of the disease include coughing up copious amounts of blood.

In the case of the Brown family, Mr. Brown had lost his wife and several children to the illness. Mercy and her brother were all that was left of his family. When Mercy died, it was winter. Her body was originally placed in a temporary crypt to be buried at a later time when the ground had thawed.

When Mr. Brown's son began to show signs of the disease, he ordered that Mercy's body be exhumed. Needless to say, she was hardly in the state of decomposition that anyone of the time would have expected. Because she remained preserved so long by the cold, her body appeared to be untainted by decomposition. Seeing what appeared to be hair and nail growth and elongated canines, Mr. Brown cut Mercy's heart out of her body. He burned the heart to ashes on a nearby stone that still sits next to her gravesite. He then fed the ashes to his sick son believing it would save him. It did not.

It was not until much later that it was determined the vampire hysteria of New England was based on a mysterious disease that no one understood at the time.

Mortal blood drinkers do exist. It is less than one percent of mortal blood drinkers that ever resort to violence or murder to get blood. Most of them have donors. The psychic vampire is far more dangerous than blood drinkers. This is a person or disembodied spirit that feeds on the life force of the living. Some occultists believe that the spirits of those who led vampiric lives, blood drinkers, or psychic vampires, remain earthbound and continue to draw energy from the living.

This is the real immortal vampire. Throughout time has been called the *mara* (Sanskrit for demon). It is where the word nightmare originated. These phantom creatures feed on the living usually in their sleep. During the attack, the victim is fully aware that they are pinned down with something invisible on top of their chest. Unable to move or scream, the victim is helpless against the paralyzing grip of the vampire.

Several years ago a woman who stayed in the Historic French Market Inn in New Orleans experienced such an attack. This was not the first time I had heard of such attacks occurring at that location. She claimed to awaken in the night to find a man laughing at her while sitting on her chest. She described a feeling of being "pinned down" and unable to move. The following morning she was clouded with confusion as to whether it was merely a dream. It is estimated by occultists that one in five individuals will suffer some form of psychic attack during their lifetime.

There are many types of spirits that feed on the living. Some steal vitality in the middle of the night while others feed on emotions. Often, these are the very same spirits that can become walk-ins, if given the opportunity. A walk-in is a spirit that possesses an individual. Some psychologists believe that many multiple personality disorder patients are actually people who have different walk-in spirits possessing them. The walk-in drives the living individual to behave in ways that they might not have prior to the attachment. Excessive alcohol or drug consumption often accompanies this type of possession. These parasitic spirits consume what they can off of their host then at the point of death, the spirit jumps into another healthier specimen to repeat the cycle.

Most victims are unaware of what is happening. Often, the victim is someone who is already weak, has low self-esteem, a substance abuse problem, or is depressed. As the walk-in takes over, the victim usually distances himself from others.

Substance abuse increases but rather than in social settings, the victim begins to indulge alone. Many of them begin to have a strange attraction to death and cemeteries. Others become more social. Depending on the spirit that is in control, some people become driven to seek out others and create drama, are emotionally needy, and attention-seekers. They prey upon the energy of those around them; it keeps them strong.

Other forms of immortal vampires are the incubus and succubus. These varieties of psychic vampire attack human victims sexually and drain them of energy. The incubus is the male, the succubus female.

These types of vampires are notorious for becoming walk-ins. They drive the human host to risky sexual situations for the sole purpose of draining life force from their partners. Telltale signs of this type of possession are individuals who are constantly in search of sexual conquests. Often viewed as sex addicts, these victims are insatiable. Completely unaware that their desires are stemming from spirit possession, they become sexual slaves to the spirit. They usually bounce from partner to partner with little or no concern for discretion or personal safety. The force within them pushes them further into the addiction. When the victim becomes sick or too weak to serve the spirit any longer, it leaves in search of new host, someone stronger. The former host is nothing more of a shell of their former self. The mind and body has been destroyed; the spirit left them shattered. They wander about aimlessly like zombies, unable to make sense of what happened to them.

Zombies!

Zombies are not something that I would ordinarily include in a book about spirits. However, over the years, especially on panel discussions, people approach me with questions. There has been a recent surge in people interested in zombies. For many, they are just as worthy a supernatural being as a vampire. Therefore, I shall address them.

The original zombie was a creation of Haitian magic. The *bokor*, Haitian magician, compounded a formula made from poisonous toads, poisonous blowfish, toxic plants, and crushed human bones. The mixture was ground up into a powder and usually inhaled into the delicate mucous membranes of the nose and mouth. The toxic concoction paralyzes the muscles. The victim cannot move nor speak but can see and hear.

Once used in earlier tribal times much as some Native Americans used peyote, the powder was used as a way to put select members into a near death state to communicate with spirits. The person would be buried with an air tube. A mock funeral would symbolize going to the land of death. Eventually, the person would be revived and relay messages from the other side. Sometimes there was oxygen deprivation or the antidote was not given in the right amount of time and neurological damage resulted.

A New Orleans *bokor*, Elmer Glover, stated that the zombie powder is used today in rural Haiti as a form of what he called Voodoo capital punishment. He went on to say that remote Haitian villages have no court system nor jails. Hardened criminals are given the zombie powder and buried just long enough to induce oxygen deprivation then revived with an antidote. The criminal is now the recipient of a somewhat herbal lobotomy. He then can be used as a slave working for the community.

Here in America, we have no such substance that can turn people into the living dead, but we do have our own versions of zombies. The American zombie is not a creation of some magical powder but by other substances and a degeneration of the soul. They are for all practical purposes the walking dead.

There are many people walking around, especially in the French Quarter, which would qualify as zombies. These people have destroyed their minds and their mortal souls with drugs, alcohol, and dabbling in dark magic. The person who was once there no longer inhabits the physical body. They are now merely hosts for discarnate evil spirits that propel them to continue through this plane. Sometimes fragments of the original self are present. In time, that spirit has gone and all that remains is a mere shell of what was.

How can you tell if someone is such an abomination? The personality is completely shattered. The individual is incapable of making any logical sense. They cannot form a concise thought much less string words together to form a sentence. They live only on a primal level: food, water, shelter, and sometimes sex.

The ones who still have some semblance of human in them may show glimpses of who they once were, but usually these individuals have little conscientiousness. Parts of them show signs of being sociopathic. Many are usually social bottom feeders taking whatever you have to give. Whether it is drugs, a free beer, free food, a loan they'll never pay back, or sex, if it's up for the taking, they're grabbing it. They often cling to the material world for all it is worth. Material gain, as long as it is given to them, seems very important.

As time progresses, the person becomes less and less human. The body still functions physically but no longer does the individual engage socially or emotionally with others. They are now full-fledged zombies.

Many might suggest that the condition is merely a deterioration of brain functioning due to drugs or alcohol and to some degree, it is. But addiction is more than a mental or emotional disease; it is a disease of spirit. It is a disconnection from one's higher self. It is this disconnection from the Divine that allows for lower vibrational beings to possess the physical body.

A new version of zombie has arisen recently: aggressive flesh eaters. In July 2011, a 36-year-old homeless Los Angeles woman grabbed a baby from a stroller and proceeded to slam the child into the handrail. Her intent was to break a leg off to eat. Fortunately, the baby was only badly bruised when the mother was able to get the child out of the woman's grip.

On May 21, 2012, an Illinois man attacked an eighteen-year-old female by biting her on her cheek. Two days later, a San Diego man bit the nose off of his cousin. Four days later, on May 26, a Miami man was found under an overpass, naked and eating the face off of a naked homeless man. The man continued to gnaw away at the victim's face as police shot six rounds into him. He was finally killed. The victim, a sixty-year-old homeless man survived, but literally had no face left. On that same evening, a Florida doctor was arrested for a DWI. The half-crazed man crashed his head against the police car partition until he broke open his skull, then proceeded to spit blood at police.

Several days later, a man in New Jersey was arrested after he had been holed up in his house. He was seen cutting himself by a family member who called the police. Authorities arrived to find the man cutting his own entrails out which he then threw at police when they attempted to subdue him.

On May 31, the most heinous of all attacks took place in San Antonio, Texas, when a young mother beheaded her three-week-old infant son and ate the child's brain. The following day a Baltimore student killed his roommate and ate his heart and brain.

Experts believe that new designer drugs are to blame for the recent onset of zombie-like attacks. People are literally frying their brains on these new synthetic drugs. Many would argue that zombies are a product of chemical alteration. But then those like myself, who see beyond the physical holding confirm that inside these individuals, something else is there, something not quite human.

Adventures in Ghost Hunting:
Case Studies

Case Study # 1 USS Alabama, Mobile, AL

In June 2003, I was contacted by Sony U.K. to be the only American in an all-British team working on the new PlayStation game, Ghost Hunter. I was asked to supply several haunted locations for use as models for the game. One location required a haunted ship. I knew that the *Alabama* would be the perfect location.

The crew brought a famous psychic, Billy Roberts, to work with me. We spent the first couple of days working in the haunted Manchac Swamp then at the Woodlands Plantation. Billy and I had an excellent rapport. On their last day of filming, we set aboard the *Alabama.*

The battleship had quite a long military history before retiring in Mobile Bay. On Christmas Eve 1944, that *Alabama* retired at Pearl Harbor for an extended dry dock period. On the morning of 4 May 1945, Japan attacked. The retired ship was reassigned to battle. The *Alabama* continued to fight until the end of World War II.

As soon as we entered the main deck of the ship, I began to hear the sounds of the large guns and I could smell gunpowder. The resonance of war rang in my head as if we had stepped back in time. Men were racing all over the deck, shells were being fired, and smoke was everywhere. I could even feel the sensation of the ship moving as if we were at sea. The scenes flashed back and forth through my mind's eye.

We went inside the ship and walked about the many different levels. I saw the image of a young man climbing a ladder from one level to another. Another apparition of a man was seen behind one of the large guns. Although nothing proved positive on film or digital for us, the memories of what I experienced psychically are as vivid as if I was there, when it all originally took place. In any location that was associated with a war, residual hauntings are inevitable. The intense energy from the trauma of war makes some of the strongest residual impressions there are.

The documentary that was made that day is still available on the Sony PlayStation II game, Ghost Hunter.

Case Study # 2 Onion Head

In December 2009, during the filming of *Haunted New Orleans* television show, a young woman named Angie who was complaining of a malevolent spirit in her home in Slidell, Louisiana, contacted me. Angie began explaining how she and her brother, Brandon, had been watching the television show *Ghost Hunters* one evening. When the show ended, the two decided to try out some of the ghost hunting techniques to see if it was real. They ventured out to a nearby cemetery off a nearby deserted country road.

She went on to tell me that Brandon had been drinking beer that evening. I interrupted her, "What did he take?"

She seemed surprised and said, "Nothing. We just went to the cemetery to see if ghosts were real."

I again asked her if he had taken anything or done anything aggressive towards the spirits in the cemetery. She assured me their actions were quite benign but ever since their visit, they had been disturbed by presences in their grandmother's home where they both lived. I agreed to pay them a visit.

Several days later, I ventured across the lake to Slidell to meet with Angie and Brandon. The home was located in a rural area of Slidell. It was a small trailer on property that the family had owned for many generations. Native American artwork covered the walls of the living room illuminated by the flickering lights on a small Christmas tree. I immediately tuned into the fact that the family had a deep familial lineage to Choctaw Indians. Native American indigenous spirits tend to become very agitated if other spirits step into their space. I felt certain that this was a large percentage of the increased activity. Something had made its way from the cemetery into their territory and they did not like it.

Five minutes into my interview with them, Brandon began explaining to me that there was a broken tomb and he had reached inside and retrieved a femur bone from it and took it home. He also explained that in his inebriated state when he left the cemetery, he opened the car doors and yelled out, "If anything is really here, prove it! Come on home with me!"

Time and time again I warn people not to engage in such challenges. That, coupled with taking a bone from a tomb, added to the spiritual can of worms he had opened. I tried to be as calm as possible as to not alarm the family. I quietly asked him, "And where is the femur bone now?"

"I brought it back and put it in the tomb as soon as we started having problems. But the problems are still here."

Brandon let me hear some EVP that he had recorded in his bedroom and also that was picked up while he recorded himself playing guitar. The sound of a little girl's voice and laughter could be heard. "But she's not the problem," he told me.

They had seen the dark, shadowy figure of a large man hovering in the hallway outside of their bedrooms on several occasions. This was a complicated situation. I had no way of knowing what followed him home and what spirits belonged on the property. I asked the two to take me to the cemetery and show me exactly where they went and what took place. We drove down winding country roads to a small private cemetery that they called

Onionhead. Of course, I asked how it acquired such an unusual name.

Angie explained, "Back in the 1950s, there was a man that people called Onionhead because his head was large and deformed and it was kind of shaped like an onion. His face was bloated and had large bulges on it. Because people made fun of him, he stayed away from town. He lived back in the woods along the river with his mother. Onionhead's mother was believed to be a witch of some type. She made homemade remedies and sold them to a nearby grocery store. Other than that, she rarely left her swamp home."

As Angie continued with the story, I noticed Brandon wandering aimlessly around the cemetery. It was obvious that he was intrigued with it. It was then that I realized that something had attached to him.

Angie went on, "At some point, a young girl's body was found in the woods. She had been strangled and raped. Everyone in town believed that Onionhead killed her. Before the police could deal with the situation legally, some of the townspeople went into the woods and found Onionhead. They hanged him from a tree then cut him up into thirteen pieces and buried him in that brick tomb over there."

She pointed into the darkness. "Days later, the police found the real killer, a drifter who had come through town. Another version of the story says that Onionhead burned a house down with several of children in it. There are many versions of the story. But they say he haunts the cemetery, that's why we call it Onionhead. All of the people who killed Onionhead died violently. At each crime scene, a note was left saying, "If you were there, I'm going to kill you too." It was signed "Onionhead."

In the 1970s, a group of kids used to come in here and conduct rituals trying to bring Onionhead up from the grave. The cemetery was closed in the 1980s because too many kids were doing rituals out here, sacrificing animals to Onionhead.

I walked over to Brandon who was hovering over the grave of an unnamed baby. "It was here," he said.

"What happened here," I asked.

I followed him with the video camera on night shot.

"I lit a candle here, for the baby," he mumbled, "Then I walked over to the brick tomb and saw that some of the bricks were missing. I looked inside with a flashlight and saw the leg bone. I crawled in and took it out."

I followed Brandon with the camcorder as he retraced his steps through the cemetery. When were finished, I told the two that I'd contact them again after deciding how to properly cleanse not only the property, but also Brandon. Later that night, when I reviewed the footage I had taken in the cemetery, I noticed that everywhere Brandon went a misty fog-like substance followed him. Angie forwarded photos she had taken that evening as well. On several photos, Brandon was covered in ectoplasm.

He definitely had something attached to him. Due to the heavy Native American presence, I contacted Phillip Humphries who was also Choctaw to conduct the cleansing.

Phillip accompanied me on the following visit. He began the cleansing by burning specially blended incense in front of and around the house. As he sprinkled the incense he chanted a prayer for protection for the family. He then had Brandon lie down on the sofa and proceeded to do a smudge cleansing over him. Then we ventured back to the cemetery.

In the cemetery, Phillip did a ceremony to calm the spirits and send back those who belonged there. We urged Brandon to discontinue visits to Onionhead Cemetery to avoid further problems with latch-on spirits. Hopefully, he took our advice and stayed away from the cemetery.

Case Study # 3 Abita Springs, Louisiana

Several years ago, my team conducted an investigation of a private home in Abita Springs, Louisiana, a rural community of the North Shore of Lake Pontchartrain. The investigative team consisted of Kriss Stephens, Jeffrey Taylor, Monte Plaisance, Jamie Cain, psychic Nora Natale, and myself. The client was disturbed by the ghost of a young boy whom she had seen repeatedly coming in and out of the front door of her home. The child had lived there at one time and was hit by a car right outside the home. We had no intention of attempting to remove this spirit, as he seemed to be quite content staying in the home. Our intent was only to document the activity and make recommendations to keep his activity from disturbing the family.

When we first set up in the location, we burned wormwood on a piece of charcoal to assist in calling up whatever spirits might be present. We kept the room dark, lit only with candles. The room quickly dropped in temperature. Nora and I walked around the house and noted that the mirrors in the family room were all on exterior walls and faced one another creating a portal for spirits to pass through. We began the task of rearranging the mirrors. While we did this, a gallon jug of water hurled off of the coffee table and onto the floor spilling everywhere.

Monte and Jamie ran over to clean up the spill. Monte noted that something brushed up against his pant leg as he walked across the room. Whatever it was left a wet spot on his jeans. Thinking it might just be water; we didn't give a lot of attention at first. When the moving of mirrors and cleaning up of water had been completed, we all sat in a circle quietly to see what might happen next. Monte complained that his leg felt sticky. We turned on the overhead lights and noted that his pant leg had a sticky, greenish slime on it. There was nothing of that consistency present so we could only assume that it was ectoplasm from the spirit brushing against him.

After about an hour of nothing happening, I decided to try an experiment to entice the ghost to interacting. I asked Jeffrey to sit in the corner of the room where some children's toys were located. I instructed him to play with the toys and talk to the little spirit, inviting him to play along. For several minutes Jeffrey pushed toy trucks around and played with blocks. Suddenly, Jamie started reciting a nursery rhyme over and over again.

"*Sing a song of six pence/ a pocket full of rye/ four and twenty black birds baked in a pie/ when the pie was opened/ the birds began to sing/ wasn't that a dainty dish to set before a king?*"

She repeated it about five times then stopped. Jeffrey looked up from the toys with a strange look on his face; he didn't look like himself. He said very calmly, "Keep singing, you're doing good."

His voice had changed. He sounded more childlike. The entire group began reciting the nursery rhyme over and over again. Jeffrey crawled all over the floor like a young child, playing and throwing blocks, and pushing around a toy fire engine. It was as if the child's spirit inhabited him. He paid no attention to the group except to tell us to keep singing. We sang the nursery rhyme to him repeatedly. Then his mood changed, and he yelled, "Stop!"

We watched as Jeffrey curled up in a fetal position in the corner and cried. When we attempted to talk to him he would scream and throw toys. Finally, Monte moved in toward him and put a hand on his shoulder. He talked quietly to the child and assured him that everything was ok. Jeffrey curled up even tighter against the corner. Monte rose up and began to walk away slowly. As he did, he felt a small hand take his. We videotaped Monte walking across the room, holding the ghostly hand, as more ectoplasm appeared on his pant leg. Then, in an instant, the spirit was gone. The room returned to normal temperature and Jeffrey sat in the corner looking around unaware of what just took place. Jeffrey felt tired but had no idea why. He claimed to have no memory of the experience or of the nursery rhyme being sung.

Interestingly, we captured no physical evidence in the form of EVP, or photographs, or video other than the slimy residue left on Monte's pant leg and Jeffrey's actions. We all know what we saw and felt but we could not really prove it. Not all investigations will provide concrete evidence. Sometimes all you have to go on is what you feel or experience in that moment. Lack of physical proof does not conclude that a haunting doesn't exist, only that it could not be documented. We concluded that in this case, the property owner should set aside a special place for the child and to allow him to have his own toys there letting him know that he was welcome.

Case Study # 4 The International School in New Orleans

One of the episodes of *Haunted New Orleans* television show featured a visit to a haunted schoolhouse in Uptown New Orleans, The International High School. School board member Andrew Ward agreed to be a part of that investigation.

We conducted a late night investigation in search of the ghost of woman believed to be a former headmistress of the school. A benevolent spirit, she watches over the children as she has for many years. Andrew had experienced sounds of footsteps and doors slamming at night during board meetings.

I waited out in front of the school for Andrew to arrive. I could feel the presence of someone watching me from one of the upper windows of the school. A sleek shadowy impression of a woman stood staring down at me then vanished as quickly as she appeared.

Andrew and I ventured up the steps of the after hours empty building and into the main classroom. I followed him with a night shot camcorder as he cautiously roamed in the darkened room. Andrew noted that the temperature gauge was jumping around sporadically. He also felt numerous cold spots. Ironically, at the same time, I was feeling very hot and claustrophobic. It was if there was very little air in the room. Suddenly, something ran into me. It knocked me forward and the camera shook. “Whoa!” I exclaimed.

It no sooner had hit me then Andrew felt something go right through him. "Oh my!" he blurted, "What was that? Did you feel that?"

I steadied the camera. "I don't know, did you feel it too?" I asked still shaken from the rush.

"It went right through me. That was really weird," he said.

"Let's follow it. It went through those doors," I pointed to the right.

We followed the strange energy through the doors and down the hallway to another classroom. I looked inside the glass in the door. I could feel her presence. "She's in there," I told him.

I led Andrew through the room to a lounge area. There was an upholstered chair next to the wall. "She's there," I insisted.

"Go sit in the chair and let's see if you channel her," I instructed.

"What? Why me?" he asked alarmed.

"You are the only other one here and I have the camera," explained, "It will be fine."

Andrew slowly moved towards the chair. "This doesn't seem right, something could go wrong," he worried.

"Just do it," I snapped.

Andrew slowly lowered himself onto the chair. "Oooooh!" he shouted, "This feels weird."

Suddenly, the auto focus on the camcorder started going in and out of focus. Andrew spoke softly to the spirit, assuring her that we meant no harm. "This feels too weird, I don't want to do this," he protested.

A couple of seconds later, the camcorder focused again and we no longer felt her presence. We later communicated with her a short while using a communication board. As we suspected, she enjoyed staying at the school, watching over the children. This is what made her happy in her life and it was here she chose to stay in after death.

As in many cases, this investigation proved to be a short one but we did have an amazing experience with the spirit in the building. Some investigations take numerous visits with no results.

Case Study # 5 LeCitron Bistro

LeCitron Bistro was another location that was investigated for the *Haunted New Orleans* television show. The restaurant is located almost directly on the river in the Lower Garden District. Chef and owner, David Baird, did extensive research of the property when he purchased the building. In this case, Mr. Baird had all documentation provided for us. It was apparent that he had done his homework.

Jesuits, who were later expelled from Louisiana in 1763, originally built the structure. It was later the home of Eleazer Wheelock Ripley, a Brigadier General in the War of 1812. Ripley lost the building in a lawsuit eventually and it was sold at public auction. The residual negative energy that resulted from both losses set the wheels of a haunting in motion. But LeCitron Bistro has an added attraction to the residual haunting; an intelligent spirit or two also inhabit the restaurant.

The owner and staff of the restaurant have documented numerous accounts of manifestations through the years. One of the bartenders experienced a menu flying across the bar and practically hitting him in the head. Both the bartender and the owner experienced the wine rack become completely rearranged after the building had been locked up overnight. Numerous employees had seen a large hooded spectral being wandering the building late at night. Lights adjust on their own, doors slam.

A waitress reported silverware drawers opening on their own.

In July 2005, David Baird entered the building and saw a large "O" on the glass on one of the doors. It first appeared that someone had drawn it on with a black marker. But upon closer examination, Mr. Baird noticed that the circle was comprised of numerous large, black flies. He immediately checked every possible source for the flies to be in the building but found nothing. He got rid of the flies but a friend warned that it was a bad omen. Hurricane Katrina hit New Orleans by the end of that following month. David Baird believes that one of the resident spirits warned him of oncoming disaster.

It was during this investigation that I used the Ovilus again. A small altar sits in an alcove where the restrooms are located. A street sign saying "Religious" sits atop. The first word that popped up was "religion." I continued to move around the altar to see what would come up next. Interestingly, the machine uttered the word, "priest". I used the machine throughout the building and in the courtyard and the only times those two words emerged, were in the altar area. I brought in paranormal investigator, Eugenia Rainey, on another visit and asked her to walk around with the Ovilus. She got the exact same words in the same area.

On the third visit, we brought in psychic Phillip Humphries to what he might pick up. We gave Phillip no background information whatsoever. When Phillip enters a haunted building he is like a racehorse darting out of the stall. He quickly takes off in different directions rattling off what he's picking up. The problem is keeping up with him. Unless one is right on him with a camera, it's impossible to document everything he is feeling and seeing. Much of which he connects to does not remain in his memory once he comes down from his trance state.

Upon entering the building, Phillip immediately stated that he envisioned something hanging from the ceiling; something to do with leather. He also pointed in several locations where the walls had been either removed or changed. David sat in a corner nodding. He apparently knew exactly what Phillip was seeing. David was amazed that Phillip had knowledge of major renovations that had been conducted over the years in the building even though he had never been at the location before.

Phillip stated that he could see leather hanging from the ceiling and smell leather. He then referenced a blacksmith shop. David confirmed that in 1819, the building was used as a blacksmith shop. He also confirmed that portion of building being used to tan leather.

Phillip went on to describe "a religious place but not a typical religion." At the time, the Jesuit order was considered somewhat unorthodox compared to other orders.

David stated, "I was very impressed. I was surprised how Phillip picked up on things that we knew from the history that he wouldn't have known."

This investigation produced evidence of multiple active and residual hauntings that have been compounded over the years. As with most investigations, there was no need to attempt to cleanse or remove any of the activity from the building. Activity was merely documented causing as little disruption as possible to the energy of the area.

Natchez Revisited

In *Tales From The French Quarter*, I, along with skeptic Allan Gilbreath, conducted a series of investigations on several properties in Natchez, MS. The main investigation took place in a large pink mansion situated on the bluff overlooking the river. A woman named Maggie owned the mansion at the time. Maggie was in her eighties when we interviewed her. Maggie's granddaughter, Megan, who was concerned about the spiritual activity going on in her grandmother's house, had called us in. There were also two other properties owned by the family that had been reputed as haunted - Sligo and Laurel Hill Plantations.

The locals called Maggie "the Witch of the Bluffs". She was a spiritualist who enjoyed having friends over for séances and spiritual readings. Maggie had a wide array of spirit visitors in her home for over fifty years. She engaged in conversations with them and listened to the stories of their lives as if she were talking to the living. These spirits were her friends and companions. Shortly after our investigation of the home, Maggie passed away.

Three years later, Megan contacted me because she claimed to be plagued by evil spirits in the house. She had become so hysterical that she was considering selling the mansion. This home had been in her family for several generations; I wasn't about to let that happen. I arranged to return to Natchez to clear out what I believed to be spirits left in the home from the days of Maggie's séances. I contacted Allan and he agreed to meet me in Natchez. This time we brought along members of a paranormal investigation organization out of Memphis: PRIA.

PRIA members Mike Wurst, Andy Brisendine, Stephen Guenther, Tanya Vandesteeg, and Allan arrived on Friday to conduct their investigation. PRIA investigates throughout the southeast U.S. Stephen Guenther described the group and its goals, "We are four very different people from different backgrounds but we just gel together perfectly as an investigative group. We have become good friends as well, enjoying our common interest in the paranormal. We balance skepticism with our desire to understand the spirit realm and are constantly trying to debunk or recreate our findings. We believe in some sort of a transition to another plane, a hereafter and that perhaps our paths do cross with ghosts, spirits and other unexplained phenomenon. If we can rule out the mundane causes, hoaxes and tricks of the eye or computer, then what is left is paranormal, which is to say is unexplainable at this time."

I arrived the next day. I pulled into the driveway and saw Allan talking to Megan's mother, Charlotte. I walked up to hear Allan explaining to her that the electrical box needed to be replaced and a complete mold removal as well. One of the issues in the home was an odd feeling in the basement and around the stairs leading to it. The electrical circuit box was at least eighty years old if not older. Many live wires were loose and hanging about giving off a very powerful electro-magnetic field. Allan explained that basically they were living in a microwave oven.

As he walked with her and opened the basement door, I immediately caught a whiff of the mold smell. “I’m not going down there,” I immediately announced.

I suffer from severe mold allergies and didn’t dare expose myself to what was in there. Allan had detected black mold in the basement three years before and it was apparent that it had only gotten worse. Allan had also pointed out issues with the electrical box on the first visit. Like the mold, it had progressed from bad to worse.

While Allan did a walk-through of the basement, I went inside the house to let Megan know that I had arrived. As soon as I walked in, I detected that the feel of the first floor was completely different from what I had previously experienced. Megan had cleared out Maggie’s belongings and replaced them with her own. The energy felt peaceful and very home-like. I quickly glanced into each room and noticed that even the mirrors had been rearranged better, cutting off any portals. I pointed out to Megan that the energy in the house was totally different and I didn't pick up anything negative. She escorted me upstairs.

As soon as I got about midway up to the second floor, I was hit with heaviness reminiscent of what the house felt like when Maggie had invited spirits in. The entire floor was cluttered with old clothing, furniture, and assorted trash. Megan led me to what the family called the Confederate Room. Maggie had mentioned on my last visit that the home had a couple of resident ghosts, one of whom was a Confederate soldier who stayed in that room. The other was a former owner who stayed confined to the attic. I wasn't concerned with either of them since they were always attached to the house and were not going anywhere. I was in search for something that didn't belong.

The other upstairs bedroom was in serious need of cleaning and painting. The bathroom didn't work and an exterior room that extended over the kitchen had been used for storage. I couldn't even walk through it. I wandered up to the attic and found the same thing. A storm had blown the attic doors open at some point and the entire room had been exposed to the elements. Old costumes and other useless items were cluttered about, much of which was mold-ridden due to excessive moisture. I had a pretty good idea of what was going on at that point. I had my plan of action in place but first we had a few other things to attend to. We took the PRIA group on a side trip to Sligo Plantation so they could try to capture activity inside the hole in the ground. While we waited for Megan to find it again, some of us walked over to a nearby pond. An old canoe lay upside down on the shore.

"There is a fifty-fifty chance that there's a water moccasin living under that canoe," Allan stated.

Unable to resist challenging him on anything, I said, "I dare you to go look."

Now, I should have known better than to dare Allan Gilbreath to do anything, especially something involving dangerous animals. The man fears nothing. I'm willing to bet that if there had been a gator out there, he would have wrestled it. Allan walked over to the boat and flipped it over. "Nope, no snake!" he yelled at me, "but there are fire ants."

He stood for a while examining the underside the boat while getting bitten by fire ants. He calmly set the boat down, eventually brushed the ants off and said, "It's not like I haven't dealt with fire ants before."

"Well, good," I mused, "now you're ready to go down and tackle some rattlesnakes and bats."

Since our previous trip, someone had covered the hole with a net to keep intruders out. The group got to go down the hole but this time all that was there were some old spider webs and leaves. We proceeded to Laurel Hill to show the group the family chapel.

The chapel at Laurel Hill was just as magnificent as it was when I first saw it three years prior. The group, being far more outdoorsy than myself, decided to walk about the wooded property in search of other interesting things.

"I'll stay here while Allan and the others go into the scary woods," I joked.

Tanya ran back several minutes later. "You have to film this!" She said enthusiastically. "There's an old cistern and all kinds of bats flying down in it. It's cool."

I paused for a moment, actually considering following her back into the woods. Then a scene from the movie, *Jeepers Creepers,* flashed into my mind. A deserted church, in the middle of nowhere, and a hole leading to who knows what with bats in it…the thought sent chills up my spine. I handed the camera over to her and asked her to not drop it down the hole. I'll take on ghosts, vampires, even the occasional demon, but creepy holes in the ground are beyond my limit. If bats are enjoying it what else might be down there? I always figure if anybody is going to have a mishap on one of these adventures, it's going to be the city girl.

When everyone returned, Megan told tales of a bigfoot-like creature being seen throughout the property. The group decided that another trip to Natchez would be necessary to try to find it. After everyone had checked themselves for ticks and removed what they could find, we headed to our next destination.

No trip to Natchez would be complete without a visit to Fat Mamma's Tamales. We had to introduce the PRIA members to Fat Mamma's for tamales and margaritas. Over dinner, we discussed their findings during their investigation and I also prepared them for what I would be doing later in the evening. At this time, I explained to Megan the importance of cleaning up the house. I didn't detect any negative entities present but there was an awful lot of negative emotional residual amongst the clutter of her grandmother's and great grandmother's belongings in the upper floors. There was also a great deal of emotional energy caused by the squabbling of family members of what belonged to whom. This was compounded by everyone's hysteria of believing there was a demon in the home. Chaotic energy was bouncing off of everyone and everything in the home.

Tanya recounted her experiences on the previous evening, "I had several personal experiences in the house during the investigation including a couple growls in one of the second floor bedrooms: Several K2 meter hits from a trapped spirit in the Confederate room and wispy lights in the boy's bedroom, but little did I know that the 'water witching' with Allan Gilbreath was going to be the highlight of the investigation. It was so interesting to feel the vibrations of the water underneath the house all the way up on the sun deck. It explains a lot of why the residents in that area are so sensitive to their surroundings."

Stephen Guenther provided me with a detailed report of Friday evening's investigation. "We drove down to Natchez and arrived Friday evening to set up and conduct our investigation prior to Kalila cleansing the home the next night. These were the nights of the super-moon full moon, adding to the mystique of this investigation. We began to set up our equipment and get ready for our investigation.

We took interior and exterior photos for our documentation and began to walk around the house to record some baseline readings with the K2 meter and a digital thermometer. Allan was with us on this initial sweep and he has terrific insight into real life causes of EMF's and other false/positives such as shiny items, which may later create a sense of reflection, or a room space built in such a way that voices might carry unusually well.

As hopeful and optimistic as we are about making contact with spirits and collecting evidence, sometimes Allan is equally hopeful in his debunking and explanations.

One example of this was during the initial sweep and taking baseline readings. We were getting some unusually high K2 readings in the basement. We had found and noted power sources and some antiquated wiring but we were getting some high readings in the middle of the basement near some old wire and an old rotary dial phone that was heaped in a pile. We were interested in this as there was no power close by; there had been other activity reported down there and we were recording readings in the surrounding area when Allan explained to us that it could be that old dusty phone and wires in the middle of the room, away from any power sources, that gave us isolated higher readings on an intermittent basis. While I can accept this as a possible explanation it seemed rather hopeful.

Later on that evening, Tanya and I were in the confederate room. There are accounts of General Robert E. Lee staying in the room and in fact the family has a button off of one of General Lee's uniforms preserved in their collection. The room is filled with civil war memorabilia, artifacts and confederate décor. There is more than one account of people outside on the property seeing the figure of a man at one of the windows in this room. Some even describe him as in uniform.

In several rooms mirrors were positioned in triangular patterns where the reflections overlapped and intersected creating the odd effect of multiple reflections and strange lines of sight. In the confederate room, one of the old mirrors was actually positioned waist high and had a chair in front of it. Sitting in that position was exactly how one would scry or look into a mirror for visions and divination. I sat in the chair facing the mirror and Tanya sat at my right in another chair. We started the digital audio recorder and also set the K2 meter on the base of the scrying mirror.

As we began to ask questions we noticed the lights moving on the K2 meter. We were getting a few hits and we asked if the spirit was trapped there and the lights blinked and we asked again for confirmation and again they blinked. We asked if we could help it move on and did not receive an answer. We knew Kalila was doing the cleansing the next night and perhaps that would help the spirit move on or be released. No EVP's were recorded but we did have positive response on the K2 for a number of questions. We were ready to move on to another room upstairs.

At least three of us independently and together reported seeing movement and the appearance of what we would refer to as the 'wispies'. Mike and Andy were in the rooms taking some readings when Andy reported seeing something. I listened. Andy is the consummate tech guy. He constantly identifies, reports, recreates, and debunks false/positive readings and situations that have a reasonable explanation.

Andy caught some movement in the old consultation rooms and followed it. What he saw was a small white ethereal movement, very fluid and graceful, white and self-illuminated. A wispy apparition moved along the floor area in the room.

Later that evening, Tanya reported the same sighting without knowledge of what Andy had seen. I caught the same thing out of the corner of my eye. It resembled the underwater movements of a translucent jellyfish but without the shape, just a thin wispy spirit moving gently through the lower regions of the room. We could not find any such shape recorded by our infrared cameras in the room.

Allan explained the geography of the area and the old house on the bluff was actually moving. We lay down on the floor of the outdoor balcony in the quiet, still air under the light of the super-moon. You could relax, close your eyes and by lying very still, actually begin to feel the powerful water running under the ground upon which the house was standing. Allan referred to this as 'water witching'.

Our bodies picked up this very subtle vibration and movement, contributing to the strange and uneasy feeling of the house.

Paranormal investigation is by definition frustrating and inconclusive. Neither believer nor skeptic can absolutely close the case on paranormal activity. For the members of PRIA our search continues."

Later that night, I walked through the entire home smudging with a special blend of incense that Phillip had put together for me. I knew in advance there were also indigenous native spirits tied to the land. Phillip, a Choctaw, knew exactly what to put together to calm down the chaos and get rid of anything that didn't belong there while simultaneously pleasing the native spirits who protect the home. In fact, he had made the mixture several months prior and had no idea why he felt the need to put it together. When I called him and explained what I needed, he said, "Oh, I have that and now I know why I made it."

That night I slept more soundly than I had in ages. A peace enveloped the house and everything felt much lighter.

The next day we completed our adventure with a trip to the Natchez Indian ceremonial mound. I had visited it several years prior when I was on my way to Vicksburg. During my previous visit, there was no one else on the mound. It had been a very hot July day. As soon as I walked across the village, I could feel spirits in the trees. When I got to the mound, the wind picked up and a cool breeze blew by. I kept seeing a black dog watching me out of the corner of my eye. It didn't seem to be harmful so I got the impression it was the manifestation of a guardian spirit. I didn't spend much time there.

The cool breeze faded quickly and the intense direct sun became a bit too much for me but I never forgot how peaceful and calming the area was. This trip was a bit different. It is always a different energy when you have more people. We formed a circle and did a simple sage smudge to remove any residual energy from all of us. Then we went our separate ways. Megan offered to take me to lunch on the Natchez Trace so I stayed a while longer.

As I had lunch with Megan, she mentioned how stressful her job was. I had never asked her what she did for a living so it seemed appropriate to inquire. She explained that she worked for the court system as a social worker. Her job was to have emotionally disturbed patients taken in for mandatory commitment orders. She also worked with families of drug addicts, alcoholics, and mentally ill patients. The final piece of the puzzle had finally fallen into place.

The situations she faced on a daily basis would have anyone seeing large dark shadows at night. I explained to her the necessity to ground herself before going to work and making sure she disperses the negative energy into the ground before returning home. I also made a list of things she could use to do regular cleanses on herself and the home. This coupled with a major cleaning of the house should remove any chaotic energy that is being disruptive. Hopefully, she followed through with my advice. As long as she continues on her current path, she risks opening the door for unwelcome entities and negative energy of others. Sometimes the things that haunt us are not those who have passed on, but emotions and negativity from those around us.

All Along The East Coast

In 2004, I decided to take a trip visiting the most haunted locations along the East Coast. I had a friend living in Rhode Island at the time so I incorporated a visit into my expedition up and down the coast.

Just a few miles into Massachusetts is the quaint town of Fall River, home to the legendary Lizzie Borden Bed & Breakfast. The legend states "Lizzie Borden took an axe and gave her mother 40 whacks. When she saw what she had done she gave her father 41". The truth is that no one really knows who killed Andrew and Abby Borden in 1892. Andrew's body was found on the sofa, slumped over. He had been hit with a hatchet-like weapon ten or eleven times. Reports indicated that one of his eyeballs had been split in half. Abby Borden's body was found in the guest bedroom. She had been hacked over twenty times with what is believed to be the same murder weapon used on her husband. Lizzie found the bodies.

She was tried for the murders. Lacking any murder weapon and solid evidence against her, Lizzie was acquitted in 1893. Despite never having been convicted, the townsfolk of Fall River continued to believe that Lizzie got away with it.

Today, the former Borden residence serves as a bed & breakfast. Guests report seeing a woman dressed in Victorian attire whisking through the house early in the morning. Some hear a woman's cry. A ghostly impression is sometimes seen on the bed in the room where Abby was killed. One of the main attractions at the B&B is that guests can order the last meal eaten by the Bordens. The Bordens murder remains a mystery and the legend of an axe wielding Lizzie lives on.

After a couple days of visiting local haunts, I hit the highway. My travels took me to Pennsylvania and the Eastern State Penitentiary, one of the most haunted prisons in the U.S. The facility opened its doors in 1829 under strict Quaker rule. It quickly became one of the most brutal penal institutions in history.

Dimly lit cells were only eight by twelve feet; barely enough room for one inmate. Apparently the state felt this was adequate given the fact that all inmates were kept in solitary confinement. A small feed slot became their only connection to the outside world. Most of them went mad due to their isolation. Torture rivaling the Inquisition was commonly practiced. A commonly used torture method was the "water bath". Inmates would be dipped in icy water then hoisted up and left dangling on the wall for sometimes hours on end. During winter months, this was particularly cruel, as the wet skin would freeze.

Another popular device used was the "mad chair". Inmates were strapped in so tightly that the slightest move cut off circulation. They were often strapped in for days at a time. But the worst of all devices was the "iron gag". A tiny iron collar was clamped onto the tongue attached to a chain that attached at the wrists. The arms were then pulled behind the back and secured tightly. The collar usually cut into the tongue causing profuse bleeding. Many inmates bled to death.

"The hole" was a pit beneath Cellblock 14. Those thrown in shared the space with bugs and rats while being fed only one slice of bread a day and a cup of water. Those inmates, who did not die from torture, went insane living hellish existences in their tiny confinements.

Al Capone spent eight months at the facility, but, somehow escaped the fate of the others. His cell was decorated, complete with a desk, a real bed, a chair, and an oriental rug.

Today the prison is a tourist attraction. Its dark, dingy cellblocks are cold, damp, and foreboding. As I walked through its corridors I could feel the desperation that echoed throughout the empty cellblocks. There is a certain emptiness that is difficult to compare to anything else but commonly experienced when I visit abandoned prisons. Shadows darted about into darkened cells. I heard odd sounds like someone moaning or sobbing in a distance. In one of the older cells, a shadow stands in a corner emanating hatred and sadness. Perhaps it is the spirit of a man that caught the attention of author Charles Dickens who visited the prison in the 1840s for a chapter in his *American Notes*.

Dickens was horrified and sickened at the treatment of the inmates. Upon seeing one inmate he described a "dark shroud, an emblem of the curtain dropped between him and the living world".

One inmate in particular made an impact on Dickens. The man had painted a mural around his entire cell. The author felt as if this individual painted his soul into his art, leaving nothing inside of him. Dickens described the man, "He is like a man buried alive, to be dug out in the slow round of years; and in the meantime dead to everything but torturing anxieties and horrible despair."

I stayed in the facility until I was exhausted from the energy. I continued onto Gettysburg.

Locals tell tales of ghostly soldiers appearing on and around the battlefield. One of the more popular spirits is that of our first President, George Washington. The legends states that the ghost of Washington appeared waging war against Confederate troops at Little Round Top. As the story goes, he appeared dressed in a uniform of the American Revolution riding a white stallion with a flaming sword raised above his head. He commanded Union troops to, "Fix bayonets! Charge!"

Union troops forced the Confederates into a full retreat. It is said that a ghostly rider upon a white steed can be seen galloping across the battlefield on hot summer nights. One of the most haunted areas of town is Sachs Bridge. Numerous people have captured apparitions of horses and the sounds of hooves crossing the covered bridge. I spent some time trying to obtain phenomena at the bridge during my investigation. I heard distant whispers and saw a few shadows in my peripheral vision. There is a strange energy felt inside. At one point, while I attempted to film, I felt as though I was being watched. A chill ran down my spine and suddenly I felt panicked. I stepped further under the bridge stepping directly into a cold spot. A strange sound emitted from above. I looked around with the night-shot camera but saw nothing. I heard something rustling above me. Feeling uneasy, I exited the bridge.

Another area that is a hotbed for paranormal activity is Devil's Den. It is the site of the heaviest fighting on the second day of battle July 2, 1863. The Native Americans named the rocky area for its infestation of rattlesnakes amongst the rocks.

Common occurrences include camera malfunctions, batteries running down, and shutters sticking. As with many actively haunted locations, once they leave the area, the cameras resume working. Locals blame this activity on photographer Alexander Gardner who photographed the area shortly after the battle. Gardner was taking photos of dead soldiers when he decided to drag one soldier's body to a location inside the den where it was more picturesque. The photograph became very famous but to this day, few people can take pictures in that spot. I challenged the legend by attempting to photograph the area. My camera locked up, refusing to cooperate. Once I left the area, the camera operated normally again.

One famous ghost of Gettysburg is that of Mary Virginia Wade (Jennie), the only civilian killed at the battle. Jennie was only twenty years old when she was shot inside her house as she made bread for the soldiers. To this day, over 150 bullet holes are seen in the side of the former Wade home. Visitors touring the house often smell the aroma of freshly baked bread in the kitchen.

As I drove down Cemetery Hill late one evening, I witnessed the opaque apparition of what appeared to be a soldier wandering alongside the road. I caught him in the corner of my eye as I drove by. When I stopped and looked again, he had vanished. In the quiet late night on the field, the sounds and smells of battle are still experienced.

The most haunted house in town is the Farnsworth House. There are no less than fourteen ghosts inhabiting what is now a bed & breakfast. The main ghost is one the proprietors call "Mary". She appears to those guests who are in discomfort. Some have felt her sitting on the bed alongside them. The ghost of a young boy is also very active. A horse and carriage outside the house killed him many years ago. He and his grieving father are commonly reported wandering about the property.

Confederate soldiers occupied the house using it as a stronghold against Union Troops. They shot from windows in the attic. It was from this location that the shots that killed young Jennie Wade were fired. Overnight guests often hear sounds coming from the attic, as if someone is moving furniture. One bathroom sometimes has blood dripping from the attic above.

It was in this tiny town that President Abraham Lincoln gave his famous Gettysburg Address. Some residents claim that his ghost haunts the Wills House where he finished writing his speech. But to hunt the ghost of Lincoln, you must really travel a bit further to our nation's capital. The last stop on my trip was to Washington, D.C. where I visited national historic sites, museums, and sought out ghostly tales.

Abraham Lincoln had a curious interest in the supernatural. It is noted that he held numerous séances in the White House in attempts to contact his son Willie who had died there. After the President's death, his widow, Mary Todd Lincoln, sought out mediums to communicate with her husband. Many who live and work in the White House have reported the ghost of Lincoln through the years. Lincoln had prophesized his own death through several dreams that he had shared with his wife. Lincoln recounted the dream to a bodyguard and friend named Ward Hill Lamon. Lamon wrote a biography on Lincoln after his assassination.

He wrote, "About ten days ago, I retired very late. I had been up waiting for important dispatches from the front. I could not have been long in bed when I fell into a slumber, for I was weary. I soon began to dream. There seemed to be a death-like stillness about me. Then I heard subdued sobs, as if a number of people were weeping. I thought I left my bed and wandered downstairs. There the silence was broken by the same pitiful sobbing, but the mourners were invisible. I went from room to room [in the White House]; no living person was in sight, but the same mournful sounds of distress met me as I passed along. It was light in all the rooms; every object was familiar to me; but where were all the people who were grieving as if their hearts would break? I was puzzled and alarmed. What could be the meaning of all this? Determined to find the cause of a state of things so mysterious and so shocking, I kept on until I arrived at the East Room, which I entered. There I met with a sickening surprise. Before me was a catafalque, on which rested a corpse wrapped in funeral vestments. Around it were stationed soldiers who were acting as guards; and there was a throng of people, some gazing mournfully upon the corpse, whose face was covered, others weeping pitifully. 'Who is dead in the White House?' I demanded of one of the soldiers 'The President' was his answer; 'he was killed by an assassin.' Then came a loud burst of grief from the crowd, which awoke me from my dream. Lincoln was killed two weeks later."

Various people over the years have claimed to see the ghost of Lincoln, including Winston Churchill. He spent one night there then refused to stay again after Lincoln's apparition appeared in front of a fireplace mantle and stared at him. But the ghost of Lincoln is not all that haunts the White House. A legend of a demon cat has plagued its halls for decades.

Tales of the black cat began back when the capital was new and cats were used in basements to control rodents. Guards claimed to witness a black cat that first appears as a kitten then grows to gargantuan proportions as it nears. Over time the cat became a harbinger of doom. Its appearance usually occurred a day before some great tragedy as it did prior to the assassinations of both Lincoln and Kennedy. Many attribute the stories to drunken guards but others swear that the cat appears. There is no way to properly document its existence nor the appearance of Abraham Lincoln's ghost. But the stories have become intertwined in our capital's history.

In addition to haunting the White House, Abraham Lincoln's ghost is believed to also haunt the Ford's Theater, where he was assassinated. Lincoln's apparition is said to be seen wandering through the theater. His assassin, John Wilkes Booth, also haunts the theater. Many have heard footsteps running toward the box where Lincoln was seated, followed by the sound of shots being fired and people screaming. Others see what is believed to be the ghost of Booth running across the stage. The theater is now the possession of the National Park Service. It displays the gun that was used to kill Lincoln along with the bloody pillow where the president laid his head.

The White Witch of Rose Hall Plantation

For years, I had told the story of Madame Delphine LaLaurie on the French Quarter Ghost Tour. On April 10, 1834, a fire occurred in a separate back kitchen of the home located at 1140 Royal Street, on the corner of Governor Nicholls Street. When firemen arrived to extinguish the fire, they found two slaves chained to the stove in the kitchen. One of them, an elderly slave woman admitted to starting the fire to bring attention to a dark secret held by Madame LaLaurie and her surgeon husband, Dr. Louis LaLaurie.

Inside a small attic crawlspace above the slave quarters, authorities found a torture chamber complete with slaves chained to the walls, obviously victims of crude medical procedures. They were emaciated and covered in scars from beatings. Most of their faces had been disfigured making them look more like gargoyles. One woman's arms had been severed and her entire face had been stripped using a scalpel. Another male victim appeared to have suffered some crude sex change operation. One woman had been shoved into a small wooden cage that might accommodate a medium-sized dog. When the cage was broken open, it revealed that her bones had been broken and set at different angles to make her fit. Many of the slaves were already dead. Those who survived were treated at Charity Hospital.

Authorities searched the home for Madame and Doctor LaLaurie, but to no avail. Apparently during the hysteria, they escaped the home disappearing at the river's edge. It is presumed that they took a ship out of New Orleans, but where? Over the years, I had heard many speculations that perhaps Delphine wound up in Jamaica taking on the alias, Annie Palmer, while continuing to torture her slaves. I set out to Jamaica to find out if the rumors could be true. I enjoy traveling throughout the Caribbean with its white sand, blue water, and the laid back atmosphere. There is no shortage of weird in the Caribbean. Most islands have turbulent histories complete with wars, pirates, and pestilence. Jamaica is considered by many to be the most haunted island in the Caribbean. It is also home of the ghost of Annie Palmer, often called the White Witch of the Island.

Rose Hall Plantation is located right outside of Montego Bay in Jamaica. The beautiful Georgian stone mansion sits high on a hill overlooking the Caribbean Coast. The stately manor is best known for its mahogany staircase, walls, floors, and ceilings. But inside its great hall resides a dark and sinister presence believed to be from the murders committed by Annie.

In 1820, Annie married John Palmer, master of the large sugar plantation known as Rose Hall. Annie, a petite woman, was born in England and spent a great deal of her life living in Haiti. It is believed that her childhood in Haiti afforded her the education in the darker arts of the magic of Voodoo. At some point in time, young Annie grew bored of her husband and began to take slaves as lovers. It is uncertain as to why and how she killed John Palmer. Some believe that he may have caught her with one of her lovers others believed she was just evil and killed him in his sleep. But he was found dead in his bed one morning under mysterious circumstances.

Annie managed to marry twice more, both times to wealthy men who had fallen victim to mysterious deaths. She took many lovers in her lifetime, most of whom were her slaves. When she grew tired of them or they displeased her, she would have them killed and buried on the property. Her slaves feared her and nicknamed her the “White Witch” because of her powerful black magic.

Annie’s overseer was a slave who was also very knowledgeable in Voodoo magic. He had promised his daughter’s hand to a young man who had become the object of his Mistress’s affections. Knowing the fate of the young man, the overseer set out to destroy the White Witch. He confronted her one day, battling her with his powerful magic. He succeeded in killing Annie but lost his life in the battle as well. Several slaves were informed of his intentions and had ritualistically prepared a tomb for her. As the legend goes, they failed to do the complete ritual, which prevented her from leaving her grave. The ghost of the evil White Witch of Jamaica continues to wander the property, possibly in search of a new lover.

Although the story of Annie Palmer does lend itself to some similarities to Delphine LaLaurie, it is impossible that they are one in the same person. Annie was killed sometime during the slave uprising in Jamaica that began in 1831 and lasted into the following year. It is documented that Delphine LaLaurie had been in New Orleans her entire life. The rumor made for some fascinating speculations on what might have happened to Delphine, but the time frames make it impossible. No one will ever know what drove either woman to commit their crimes. All that is known is that both houses remain haunted by their victims and the evil presence left behind from the bitter, angry madams.

Curses!

Some places or objects are beyond haunted; they are believed to be cursed. A cursed object or locations are situations in which evil supernatural forces affect those who come in contact with them. Some curses can be explained, as with the case of the most famous American cursed object, The Hope Diamond. As the legend goes, a French jeweler named Tavernier traveled to India in 1642. During his visit, he stole a large blue diamond from a sacred statue of the Hindu goddess Sita. It was believed that stealing from an idol unleashed certain curses upon all those who possessed the stolen item. Tavernier returned to France in 1668 and presented the diamond to King Louis XIV, after whom Louisiana is named. He wore the diamond around his neck during his reign. Tavernier was later killed by wild dogs while traveling in Russia.

The king and his wife, Marie-Therese, had already lost two children during childbirth. In 1671, their son Philippe, died at age three. One year later, a daughter, named after her mother, died at age five, along with their newborn son. Marie-Therese died in 1683. Their only living child, Louis, the Dauphin or crown prince, died in 1711. The crown went to Louis XIV's grandson, Louis XV, duc d'Anjou.

The diamond remained in the royal family until the beheadings of Louis XVI and Marie Antoinette.

The blue diamond resurfaced publicly in 1813. It was purchased in the early 1900s by a London banker named Henry Thomas Hope, whereupon it became known as the Hope Diamond.

The diamond changed owners several times over the following years. *Washington Post* owner Edward McLean acquired the famous gem in 1922 from a Turkish nobleman who had recently bought the jewel from a diamond dealer. Shortly after the dealer delivered it, he was killed in a car accident. Believing the diamond was cursed; the Turk opted to sell it. McLean, not believing in superstitions, gave it to his wife, Evelyn Walsh McLean, as a gift.

Having some knowledge of its curse, Evelyn had a priest bless the diamond before she ever wore it. Nonetheless, tragedy engulfed her life. Her nine-year-old son, Vinson, was killed in a freak car accident. Shortly thereafter, in 1933, she and Edward divorced. The courts committed Edward to a mental facility for where he remained for the rest of his life. He died of a heart attack in 1941. Five years later, their only daughter committed suicide with an overdose of sleeping pills. Evelyn, grief stricken, died one year later. Upon her death, the Hope Diamond was sent to the Smithsonian Institution in Washington, D.C. where it remains on "permanent" loan.

Clearly, this curse stemmed from the theft of a sacred object that should have never been touched from the start. Other curses have unknown origins leaving only speculation. Some of the most famous curses are found in Hollywood. Certain movies and even characters have been tainted by alleged curses bringing death and unfortunate accidents onto those associated with them. Many of them revolved around themes of occult activity or an evil persona. One of the most famous was the curse of "Poltergeist". It was believed that the curse because real due to cadavers being used in the swimming pool scene rather than props. Disrespect for the dead would certainly open a door for bad karma.

Between the beginning of filming of the first *Poltergeist* and the end of filming for the third, four cast members died. The first was Dominique Dunne, who played the oldest daughter in the original *Poltergeist.* Dunne was twenty-two when her boyfriend murdered her, not long after the first movie was released. Over the next six years, three other cast members died. Julian Beck and Will Sampson died two years apart after appearing in the second *Poltergeist.* Both died from diseases of the digestive system. Twelve-year-old Heather Rourke died from a digestive disease after appearing in all three movies.

Many people believed it was a curse to blame for the heinous murders of Sharon Tate and her friends. She was almost full term in her pregnancy when members of the Charles Manson family broke into her home at 10050 Cielo Drive in Los Angeles. One year prior to the murders Tate's husband, director Roman Polanksi, released "Rosemary's Baby," a film about a young woman giving birth to the son of Satan. The film's producer, William Castle, believed there was a curse. Shortly after production, Castle fell ill with severe gallstones. After several painful months of treatments, he finally had surgery. A short time later, the film's composer, Krzysztof Komeda, died in an accidental fall, followed by the Sharon Tate murders. In researching the Manson murders, it would seem that a weird set of coincidences rather than a curse would be to blame.

Tate and Polanski rented the home directly after its former tenants, Terry Melcher and his girlfriend, Candice Bergen, moved out. During the previous year, Melcher had severed connections with would-be songwriter, Charles Manson. Beach Boy Dennis Wilson had introduced Melcher to Manson. Wilson had picked up a couple of women who were hitchhiking, members of Manson's family, and brought them to his home. A few hours later, he found himself giving refuge to the entire Manson clan. At first Wilson showed an interest in Manson's music, introducing him to Melcher.

Melcher, too, was interested in the beginning but abandoned Manson after witnessing his unacceptable behavior. Manson had on occasion visited Melcher at his home on Cielo Drive. Shortly after he dropped Manson, Melcher and Bergen moved out of the house and the Polanski's moved in. It seemed that the tragic death of Sharon Tate and her houseguests had more to do with being in the wrong place at the wrong time rather than a movie curse.

One eerie detail about the Tate murders was that Sharon Tate allegedly had a premonition of her own demise. One of the murder victims of the Manson family was her former boyfriend, hairdresser Jay Sebring. Three years before their murders, the actress stayed alone in Sebring's home on Eaton Drive. MGM executive Paul Bern, who had been married to Jean Harlowe, had once owned the house. In 1932, Bern shot himself in the home, leaving nothing more than a cryptic suicide note. Harlowe died mysteriously of kidney failure at twenty-six years old five years later. Sebring believed the house to be haunted by Bern.

On the evening Sharon Tate stayed alone in the house, she was awakened by what she described as a "creepy little man" entering her room. He shuffled about as if he was searching for something, ignoring Tate's presence. The frightened actress fled the room and leapt down the stairs where she saw another apparition. She described a bloody body tied to the railing with its throat slit. Unbeknownst to her at the time, it was a foreshadowing of what was to come.

Another popular occult film that gained notoriety for being cursed was "The Exorcist". The original novel by William Peter Blatty was based on a true story of a thirteen-year-old boy in Maryland in 1949. The boy underwent over thirty exorcisms conducted by several clergy before being free of the demonic force that resided in him.

The original set for the MacNeil home burned down. There was no physical explanation for the fire that delayed production for six weeks. A priest was brought in to bless the rebuilt set. During the filming of the original movie, nine people were killed and others injured. Ellen Burstyn, who played Chris MacNeil, Ragan's mother, was injured during the scene where she was thrown across the room. Burstyn fell on her tailbone in the fall. Her scream of agony heard in the film was real and the injury to her spine was permanent. Linda Blair also suffered spinal injuries when a prop failed during the filming of her thrashing around in the bed.

Actors Jack MacGowran, who played Burke Dennings, and Vasiliki Maliaros, who played Father Karras's mother, both died after appearing in the film where their characters died.

Evangelist Billy Graham was convinced that evil resided in the film itself. Many believers contended that merely writing a book or producing a movie about satanic possession was enough to conjure demonic forces. Yet books and movies are not the only recipients of curses; sometimes, the characters themselves are cursed.

Just about everyone in Hollywood is familiar with the Superman curse. Some talent agencies blamed the curse for their difficulty in casting the role. George Reeves who played the character in the television show, "The Adventures of Superman," died under mysterious circumstances at the age of 45. His death was ruled a suicide, but his fingerprints were not on the gun that was found with his body. Many years later Christopher Reeve, playing the super hero in several movies, became paralyzed in an equestrian accident then died nine years later. His widow, Dana Reeve despite never having been a smoker, died at age 44 of lung cancer. Lee Quigley, who played an infant Superman, died at 14 of solvent abuse.

Margot Kidder, who played Lois Lane in several Superman movies, suffered from severe bi-polar disorder. Several people who were connected with the production of the new DVD, "Superman Returns", suffered injuries from freak accidents. One fell down a flight of stairs, another was mugged and beaten, and one was thrown through a plate glass window.

Another super hero curse taints the Batman movies, but this time it's the villain who is cursed. The Joker character is said to bring curses to those who portray the character. The original character in the 1950s comic book was a psychotic killer and Batman's first enemy. The Comic Book Code Authority forced Batman creators, DC Comics, to tone down the character to make him less frightening. Cesar Romero played the diluted version of the Joker in the 1960s *Batman* television series. Romero never felt comfortable with the role and battled with it for years. Then the character emerged in the movie, *Batman*, with Jack Nicholson as the Joker. Nicholson was no stranger to playing psychos but found the role of the Joker quite disturbing. Nicholson began to have bouts of anxiety, restlessness, and disturbed sleep which he blamed on the character. Later, Mark Hamill, who played the voice of the Joker in the animated series, reported having the same experiences as Nicholson. Like Romero, Hamill never felt comfortable with the character.

When Heath Ledger accepted the role of the Joker in "The Dark Knight," Nicholson warned him of getting too close to the character. Immediately Ledger began to suffer from insomnia and anxiety. Within a few months, he was dead from an overdose of prescription sleep medication.

One of the most famous celebrity curses is associated with a song. The Curse of the Crossroads began in the early 1900s with a Mississippi blues guitarist named Tommy Johnson.

Johnson claimed, "If you want to learn how to play anything you want to play and learn how to make songs yourself, you take your guitar and you go to where a road crosses that way, where a crossroad is. Get there, be sure to get there just a little 'fore 12:00 that night so you'll know you'll be there. You have your guitar and be playing a piece there by yourself.... A big black man will walk up there and take your guitar and he'll tune it. And then he'll play a piece and hand it back to you. That's the way I learned to play anything I want."

Sometime later, another Mississippi blues man, Robert Johnson (no relation) wrote the song *Crossroads Blues*. Robert Johnson was down on his luck and desperate for fame and fortune. After losing his wife, Virginia, and their unborn son in childbirth, in 1935, he had hit an all-time low. In a desperate attempt to become a star he traveled to a crossroads in Rosedale, Mississippi where legend has it he made a pact with Satan. As the story goes, Johnson having nothing left to lose, offered up his soul to the devil in exchange for musical ability.

Johnson's musical career soared but only for a couple of years. He recorded *Crossroads Blues* in 1936. Just two years later he was murdered. Johnson's fame was short-lived but the *Curse of the Crossroads* lived on.

Numerous musicians have recorded the song, all of which suffered tragedies shortly thereafter. Eric Clapton recorded his version of the song with the group Cream in 1968. The band broke up by the end of that same year. Clapton fell deep into the abyss of heroin addiction. Several years later, his young son died by falling out of a window of a high-rise apartment building.

The Allman Brothers band began performing the song in 1965. In 1971, Duane Allman was killed in a motorcycle accident at a crossroads. Just a year later, band member Berry Oakley was also killed in a motorcycle accident within a mile of where Duane lost his life. In the song "Melissa" Greg Allman sang, "Crossroads will you ever let him go? Or will you hide the dead man's ghost?"

Lynyrd Skynyrd performed their own version of the song throughout the mid-1970s. Their career ended in 1977 when private jet crashed into a swamp killing two of the band members as well as the plane's crew. Others who were believed to been touched by the curse were Led Zeppelin and Kurt Cobain.

Are these celebrity curses real? Many believe that they are. Still others contend that it is the belief in the curse that creates it. Sometimes what we believe becomes our reality. If one believes that they are cursed, the belief creates a cursed existence. It is a self-fulfilling prophecy that becomes true only because it is believed so strongly. Sometimes it's best to avoid such situations, places, and things that are rumored to be cursed, just in case.

Closing

It is my intent that the contents herein be a valuable to tool to those who want to hunt ghosts, heighten their psychic awareness, or simply deal with their own encounters with the paranormal. For the avid ghost hunter, please remember that going into haunted locations can open up the possibility of having spirits attach to you and winding up in your home. Try your best to know what situation you are walking into before beginning any investigation. The more preventative measures you take to protect yourself from any negative energy, the better.

Always remember to properly ground yourself before entering a haunted location. Use the meditation exercises outlined to keep you grounded and centered. If a situation does not feel right, it's best to abandon the investigation until you feel up to it or discover more about the property. If ceremonial magic practices were used in an area, it is best to seek advice from the proper clergy to clear the property before tampering with what might in there. It is equally important to do a good cleanse after. It is also advisable to make sure that your equipment is sage smudged periodically to remove any residual energy that it might have picked up. Sage and cleanse your own home and your equipment regularly. It's very easy to pick up residual energy from other locations and take it home with you. Most hauntings are not intelligent spirits. Negative residual energy can be equally detrimental.

Keep things in perspective. Remember that your intent should be merely to document the activity and to possibly connect the dots in the history of the location. You are not able to remove spirits that chose to remain attached. Also, remember that every place was something else before what it is today. Many haunted locations have indigenous spirits attached to the land. Trying to play exorcist or attempting to move them on could only aggravate the situation and possibly rile the spirits. It's always better to explain ways to a homeowner so that they can keep the spirit happy rather than play hero and try to remove it. The only time a spirit can be removed is if it does not belong there. This applies to spirits that latch onto you and follow you home. Generally, these types of spirits will eventually wander back to where they came from most of the time. If not, a good cleanse should send them on their way.

I hope that the information in this book has been helpful whether you are seeking ghosts as a hobby, trying to communicate with a loved one who has passed or just interested in what "might be". Hopefully, those who have spent years feeling as if they "were crazy" or "have a vivid imagination" will take comfort in knowing that spirits are among us. They watch us, they contact us, and every now and again, we are blessed with being able to see into their world. Keep an open mind, expect the unexpected, and may you enjoy your own search for spirits.

Parapsychology Terms

Altered State of Consciousness (ASC)- A term used to refer to any state of consciousness that is different from "normal" states of waking or sleeping. ASCs include hypnosis, trance, ecstasy, psychedelic and meditative experience. ASCs do not necessarily have paranormal features.

Apparition- The visual appearance of an entity whose physical body is not present. Generally, an apparition applies to any form of entity where it is distinguishable as a person or animal. The apparition can appear in partial or full-bodied.

Apport / Asport - An *apport* is a solid object that seemingly appears from nowhere in the presence of a medium. *Asport* is any object the 'spirits' or medium makes disappear or teleports to another location.

Astral Body - The body a person seems to occupy during an out-of-body experience.

Astral Plane - A world some people believe exists above the physical world.

Astral Projection - An out-of-body experience.

Astrology - A theory and practice, which attempts to identify the ways in which astronomical events are correlated with events on earth.

Aura - A field that some psychics see surrounding the living body.

Automatic Writing - Writing without being aware of the contents, as when a medium apparently transcribes written messages from disembodied spirits.

Automatism - Any unconscious and spontaneous muscular movement caused by 'the spirits': (Automatic writing).

Bilocation – Being (or appearing to be) in two different places at the same time.

Card Guessing - An experimental tests for ESP in which subjects guess the identity of a set of cards.

Cerebral Anoxia - Lack of oxygen to the brain, often causing sensory distortions and hallucinations. Sometimes used to explain features of the near-death experience.

Chakra- An energy center in the human body, which processes psychic energies and abilities.

Channeling - The process by which a medium apparently allows a spirit to communicate through his or her person.

Clairaudience - Auditory form of ESP

Clairsentience - Physical sensations (or smell) form ESP.

Clairvoyance - A subset of ESP. The viewing of distant scenes not apparent to the eye, may appear externally - either replacing the normal visual scene (visions) or being incorporated into it (as could be the case with apparitions) – or internally, in the form of mental imagery and intuition.

Closed Deck - A set of cards used in a card-guessing test where each card appears a fixed number of times. Statistical analysis of research data using a closed deck differs from statistical analysis of data using an open-deck.

Cold Reading - A technique using a series of general statements, questions, and answers that allows fake mediums, mind readers, and magicians to obtain previously unknown information about a person. (Reader has no prior knowledge).

Collective Apparition - An unusual type of 'ghost' sighting in which more than one person sees the same phenomenon.

Control - In experimental parapsychology a procedure undertaken in order to ensure that the experiment is conducted in a standard fashion and so that results are not unduly influenced by extraneous factors.

Crisis Apparition - An apparition is seen when the subject is at the point of death or is the victim of a serious illness or injury.

Curse - To speak a wish of evil against someone or call down forces to hurt someone.

Demon - An evil spirit that was never human.

Discarnate - Spirits that exist without a physical body.

Ectoplasm - A substance, which emanates from the body of a medium during a trance. This often appears as a mist-like substance.

Electromagnetic Field - A field propagated by a combination of electric and magnetic energy, which radiates from radio and light waves to gamma and cosmic rays. It is believed that when spirits manifest, they create an electromagnetic field.

EMF Detector - An instrument that measures electromagnetic energy. Also known as a Gauss Meter or magnetometer.

ESP - ESP or extrasensory perception is considered what scientists refer to as a receptive psi. This type of experience usually involves the transfer of information.

EVP - Electronic voice phenomena - Voices captured on audiotape when no one is present. It is believed that these voices are from spirits attempting to communicate with living people.

Experiment - A test carried out under controlled conditions.

Experimental Group - A group of subjects who undergo a specific experimental procedure. Often results from this group are compared with those of a control group.

Experimental Parapsychology - Parapsychology research involving experimental methods rather than survey techniques or the investigation of spontaneous cases.

Experimenter - The person who conducts the experiment.

Experimenter Effect - Influence that the experimenter's personality or behavior may have on the results of an experiment.

False Awakening - An experience in which a person believes he or she has woken up, but actually is still dreaming.

Forced Choice Experiment - An experiment in which the subject is forced to choose among an assortment of possible targets, such as the five ESP cards.

Free Response Experiment - An experiment in which the subject knows only the general nature of the target.

Ghost - A form of apparition, usually the visual appearance of a deceased human's 'spirit soul' or that of a crisis apparition.

Ghost Hunt / Ghost Investigation - A ghost hunt is an informal attempt to simply sight or record a 'ghost' in a location similar to others known to be haunted. A ghost investigation, on the other hand, is a carefully controlled research project, set up to record paranormal activity, usually at a location known, or presumed to be haunted.

Goat - A subject in an experiment who does not believe in the ability for which he or she is being tested.

Hallucination - Perception of sights, sounds, etc., that is not actually present. Ghosts, as we define them, are not hallucinations, because they have a real, external cause.

Hauntings - Recurrent sounds of human activity, sightings of apparitions, and other psychic phenomena, in a location when no one is there physically.

Hypnosis - State like sleep in which the subject acts only on external suggestion.

Illusion - A distorted perception of objects or events causing a discrepancy between what is perceived and what is reality.

Intuition - The non-paranormal ability to grasp the elements of a situation or to draw conclusions about complex events in ways that go beyond a purely rational or intellectual analysis.

Kirlian Photography - A photographic method involving high frequency electric current, discovered by S.D. & V. Kirlian in the Soviet Union. Kirlian photographs often show colored halos or "auras" surrounding objects.

Laying on of Hands - A process by which certain healers profess to be able to heal patients by touch.

Levitation - The lifting of physical objects by psychokinesis (PK).

Life Review - Flashback memories of the whole of a person's life often associated with the near-death experience.

Lucid Dreaming - Dreaming in which the person is aware that the experience is a dream. Often associated with feelings of aliveness and freedom, and with the ability to control dream events.

Materialization - The deliberate, usually temporary, visible and/or physical formation of a spirit.

Medium - A psychic through who spirits can communicate.

Metaphysics - Derived from the Latin word "meta" which means "beyond," metaphysics would literally mean that which is beyond the laws of physics: The study of psychical research.

NDE - Near death experience. Experienced when the person is in fact clinically dead for a period of time. The person usually feels he or she leaving their body and sometimes observing the location and people around them, they usually often view their own lifeless bodies, then the person feels as though they are rising up through some sort of tunnel towards a bright light. Sometimes they may see or hear a deceased family member or friend, or even a religious figure of some kind. The person having this experience is usually told it is not the right time, or they decide themselves it is not time to die, and they return to their bodies.

OBE - Out of body experience, or astral projection: This is the sensation or experience many people have of actually leaving their body for a period of time, this is where the spirit or soul leaves the body. This can also be described as "traveling clairvoyance."

Orb - A sphere of electromagnetic energy produced by spirits.

Ouija Board - Game board manufactured by the Parker Brothers Company. Used to communicate with spirits. Some believe this "communication" is caused by the collective unconscious of the participants.

Paranormal - Occurrences that take place outside the natural order of things. This would include ghosts, UFO's, ESP and other things difficult to explain by nature but in the realm of the natural.

Parapsychology - The branch of science that studies psychic phenomena.

Percipient - A person who sees an apparition or ghost.

Phenomenology - An approach to research that aims to describe and clarify a person's own experience and understanding of an event or phenomenon.

Poltergeist - A German word meaning 'noisy or rowdy ghost'.

PK (Psychokinesis) - The power of the mind to affect matter without physical contact.

Place memory - Information about past events that apparently is stored in the physical environment.

Precognition - The ability to predict things beyond present knowledge.

Psyche - The Greek word for "self", "mind", or "soul".

Psychic - A person with above average ESP abilities.

Psychic Healing - A mode of healing affected by the psychic abilities of the healer.

Psychic Surgery - The supposed ability to paranormally perform invasive surgery using no conventional medical tools.

Psychometry - ESP of events associated with inanimate objects.

Quantitative Method - A research method involving the collection and statistical analysis of numerical data.

Qualitative Method - A research method involving the collection of non-quantitative data (e.g., observations, interviews, subjective reports, case studies).

Remote Viewing - Another term for clairvoyance: ESP procedure in which a percipient attempts to become aware psychically of the experience of an agent who is at a distant, unknown target location.

REM - Rapid eye movement during sleep that indicates dreaming.

Repressed Psychokinetic Energy - A theoretical psychic force produced, usually unconsciously, by an individual undergoing physical or mental trauma. When released, the power causes paranormal occurrences such as poltergeist activity.

Retrocognition - The awareness of objects and events that existed in a past time

Sceptic (skeptic) - A person inclined to discount the reality of the paranormal and to be critical of parapsychological research. Generally seeks rational or scientific explanations for the phenomenon studied by parapsychologists.

Scrying - A term used to cover a wide range of divination techniques which parapsychology would tend to classify as types of ESP. Most scrying techniques involve some degree of fixation on a surface with a clear optical depth or on an area, which shows random patterns, the idea being that subconscious information available to the scrying will be manifested in their interpretation of the imagery or random patterns they see.

Séance - A group of people who gather in an effort to communicate with the dead.

Sensitive - A person with psychic abilities.

Shadow Ghost - A black, mist like spirit that has no discernable features. It is sometimes demonic in nature and is sometimes described by witnesses as a black shape.

Shaman - A 'wizard' in tribal societies who is an intermediary between the living, the dead, and the gods.

Spirit Photography - A spirit photograph captures the image of a ghost on film. Many of these are supposedly intended as a mere portrait of a living human being, but when the film is developed, an ethereal ghostly face or figure can be seen hovering near the subject. This may also incorporate orbs, vortexes, and mists to some degree.

Spiritualism - A belief system that 'spirits' of the dead can (and do) communicate with living humans in the material world.

Subjective Apparitions - Apparitions or phenomena that are hallucinations created by our minds.

Stigmata - Unexplained markings on a person's body that correspond to the wounds of Christ.

Supernatural -Something that exists or occurs through some means other than any known force in nature. As opposed to paranormal, the term 'supernatural' often connotes divine or demonic intervention.

Telekinesis - The paranormal movement of objects.

Telepathy - The direct passing of information from one mind to another.

Teleportation - A kind of paranormal transportation in which an object is moved from one distinct location to another, often through a solid object such as a wall.

Temporal Lobe Activity - Electrical activity in the temporal lobes of the brain; Often associated with strange sensations, time distortions and hallucinations. Sometimes used as an explanation for seemingly paranormal experiences such as apparitions.

Thought Form - An apparition produced by the power of the human mind.

Trance - A sleeplike state in which there is a change of consciousness.

Vortex (vortices) - A photographed anomaly that appears as a funnel that is not seen at the time of the photograph that supposedly represents a ghost.

White Noise - A hiss-like sound, formed by compiling all audible frequencies.

Bibliography

New Orleans Ghost, Voodoo & Vampires, Kalila Smith, deSimeon Press, 1997, 2004, 2007, 2009, 2012

History and Mystery: The Macabre World of New England and Beyond, Raquel Digati, Aventine Press, 2004

Recollections of Abraham Lincoln, Ward Hill Lamon

The Vampire in Europe: True Tales of the Undead, Gramercy, June 29, 1996

Vampires, The Occult Truth, Konstantinos, Lewellyn, 2002

Vampires, Death, and Burial, Paul Barber, Yale University Press, September 10, 1988

Times-Picayune, October 25, 1989, "Historic Haunts: A Halloween Visit with Ghosts in the Quarter", Millie Ball

The Unquiet Dead, Dr. Edith Fiore; Ballantine Books

Tales From The French Quarter, Kalila Smith, Kerlak Publishing

Life After Life, Raymond A. Moody; Mockingbird Press

Beyond Death's Door, Maurice Rawlings, M.D.; Bantam Books, 1971

Paranormal Experience and the Survival of Death, Carl B. Becker; State University of New York Press, 1999

Buckland's Book of Spirit Communications, Raymond Buckland, Llewellyn Publishers, Boston Journal, November 23, 1904

Principles of Nature, Andrew Jackson Davis

The History of Spiritualism, Arthur Conan Doyle

Encyclopedia of Psychic Science, Nandor Fodor,

Ghost Stories of Pennsylvania, Dan Asfar, Ghost House Pub, 2002

The Bell Witch: the Full Account, Pat Fitzhugh, Armand Press, 2000

Lessons in Becoming Myself, Ellen Burstyn, Riverhead Hardcover, 2006

The Sixth Degrees of Helter Skelter, documentary, Scott Michaels, 2009

The Curse of the Joker, Vanessa Bronson, July 2008

About the Author

Follow world-renown author and para-normal investigator Kalila Smith into the mysterious world of spirits. This book is the most concise "how to" manual for anyone who enjoys a good ghost hunt. Learn the history of spiritualism. Find out what is a ghost; what is not. Learn the truth about poltergeists. Discover how to conduct a paranormal investigation or a communication session with the dearly departed. Find out what pitfalls to avoid when investigating a haunted location.

Delve into the realm of spiritual beings that were never human. Explore the world of demons, real vampires, and join in real case studies conducted by Kalila. Taken from her paranormal class at University of New Orleans, many of the case studies have been featured on A&E, Discovery, and Travel Channel television broadcasts. This book will answer any question you have ever had about ghost hunting. It is a must have for everyone from the novice to experts. Completely updated and in its second edition, this is one of the first concise guides for hunting ghosts based on actual first hand experiences.

Kalila was born and raised in New Orleans. She personally researched and wrote the material featured on *Haunted History Tours of New Orleans' Ghost, Vampire and Spellbound* tours. She is the author of *New Orleans Ghosts, Voodoo, & Vampires, Tales From The French Quarter*, and *Miami's Dark Tales*.

She has been featured on and worked behind the scenes on television productions including *Travel Daily*, *Places of Mystery, Secret New Orleans, Unsolved Mysteries, FEAR!, MTV's On The Road, Blind Date, Hidden New Orleans, Urban Legends, America's Most Haunted Places, In Search of..., and Supernatural Destinations*. She appeared in the motion picture, *The St. Francisville Experience*. She wrote and directed *Journey Into Darkness... The Trilogy*, a video documentary, featured in segment in television broadcast in the US & UK and worked on and appeared in the documentary for Sony's Playstation II game, *Ghosthunter*. She conducted all of the paranormal investigations for the local television show, *Haunted New Orleans*. She was a producer in the PBS documentary *Southern Haunts* New Orleans episode produced by Sky Dive Films.

www.ingramcontent.com/pod-product-compliance
Lightning Source LLC
LaVergne TN
LVHW011323080426
835513LV00006B/178

* 9 7 8 1 9 3 7 0 3 5 7 1 6 *